GW00708173

Why a man should be well-dressed

Adolf Loos

Why a man should be well-dressed

Appearances can be revealing

Translated by Michael Edward Troy

Metroverlag

content

Adolf Loos, holding his ear trumpet (1929).

Intro

When I was first approached with the daunting task of translating this compilation of writings by Adolf Loos into English I was awestruck, as well as filled with more than a bit of apprehension – not really sure if I, or anyone today, really could do justice to this fascinating historical figure and his unique thoughts on a great variety of subjects. But, after reading various German publications of this great architect's and thinker's work, I came to the conclusion that an English version of these writings would introduce a whole new audience to this astute observer and innovator as well as providing fascinating insight into his life and turbulent times.

Vienna at the turn of the 20th century was a bustling metropolis, the center of the vast Austrian Hungarian Empire and a melting pot of cultures and ethnic groups. This unique diversity made the capital of this empire into one of the most fascinating and innovative cities in the world. However, a good deal of the old was still prevalent. Many of its more conservative citizens resented any changes, preferring to dwell in the glories of the past. The Austrian Hungarian Empire had, since the 1860s, been undergoing far-reaching social changes; Classical Liberalism was finding more and more acceptance. Politicians, intellectuals, artists and many entrepreneurs were engaging these newfound politics and ideas with great enthusiasm. However, this is not to say that all things new were necessarily better or even inspired, as evidenced by the observations in this book. On first review this period in history appears very different than the times of today – and it was. Yet, there are arguably many similarities as well. It was a time of rapid change, social upheaval and major technological advances. Art and music were affected by these changes, inspiring many artists to try new approaches to their craft. New influences abounded and, apparently, not all were good as evidenced by the observations of Mr. Loos.

The essays in this book, written over a span of almost thirty years therefore, in one way or another, reflect the social transformation and historical occurrences taking place. Even though many of these essays were conceived almost one hundred years ago, it is quite astounding how many of these percipient musings still have relevance today for they are not only valuable historical images but also stimulating intellectual reflections.

Fully understanding the content of this book probably requires the reader to be somewhat acquainted with Fin de Siècle Vienna and the many changes taking place during this volatile time. Yet, there is much written here that in its basic substance reflects more on core human characteristics than any particular time period. Or, as in the words of Cicero; *History is the witness that testifies to the passing of time; it illuminates reality, vitalizes memory, provides guidance in daily life, and brings us tidings of antiquity.*

Loos was a man intent on looking at change not as an absolute necessity, but rather as developments that require careful attention – and they still do.

Michael Edward Troy
Vienna, March 2011

Praise for the present

When I pass review over the past thousands of years and ask myself in which age would I like to have lived, I would most certainly say, here and now. Oh, I am sure there always has been a certain zest for life. Every era had its share of advantages. It is entirely possible that one lived happier in these times than today. But during no other time could one dress as nicely, well and practically as today.

The idea that I would have to drape myself in a toga every morning, and to have this drapery hanging around me throughout the day – the entire day, please! – in the same folds, this uncomforting thought is enough to drive me to suicide. I like to walk, walk, walk and when, on a whim, I decide to run after a streetcar racing by, the thing would surely become independent. The Romans never walked. They just lounged around. And should I wrap myself in a towel after a bath, it is certain to be located somewhere else within five minutes. I just don't have the nerves for that kind of aggravation.

However the Cinquecento, the Italian Renaissance of the 16th Century, now that is very appealing time. But, by adorning myself in silks and satins I would end up looking like a fairground fool. No thank you.

I have only praise for my clothes. They actually are the earliest human outfit. The materials are the same as the cloak Woden, the mythical Norse leader of the "wild hunt", wore. The theater tailors dye it red or blue, but it most likely it was a Scottish plaid. Because even in those times there were black sheep, and their wool blended with that of the white sheep produced the first salt & pepper weaves.

It is mankind's primeval dress. Which traveler to continents far and wide has not experienced the great disappointment when they realize that they have been fooled regarding picturesque costumes? The vagabonds in Tigris, Chicago, in China and in Cape Town are all dressed in a similar way to those at home. Even the beggar in the days of Semiramis wore the same uniform as his contemporary counterpart in Posemukel (Hicksville).

It is mankind's primeval dress. Our old pants can, regardless of the era and the area of the globe, cover the nakedness of the pauper without adding a foreign note to the time or the landscape. This dress is not something modern. It has always been with us, it has accompanied us throughout the millennia. Many great historical figures despised them, making them the brunt of stupid jokes and dehumanizing jaunts. But a destitute vagabond was and remains, in an objective visual way, aesthetic – a Louis the XIV never. I do, however, wish to stress, only for the eye and not the nose.

It is the primeval dress. It is not an invention. It did not evolve. It has always been with us, even at the naissance of human kind. From the mother lobe it rose and has remained.

It is the dress of those rich in spirit. It is the dress of the self-reliant. It is the attire of people whose individuality is so strong that they cannot bring themselves to express it with the aid of garish colors, plumes or elaborate modes of dress. Woe to the painter expressing his individuality with a satin frock, for the artist in him has resigned in despair.

When the English set it upon themselves to rule the world, they freed themselves from the imitation of the silly costumes that they had been condemned to by other nations, and imposed the primeval dress around the globe. The nation of Bacon and William the Great, the Swan of Avon, had faithfully preserved the fabrics over the millennia. The form was shaped into a single form, the uniform, in which the individual personality can best conceal its riches. It became a disguise.

It is the attire of the Englishman. It is the dress of a nation that, of all nations, counts the strongest personalities among its population. A nation where the tough individual without means, the vagabond, is not locked up or put in a workhouse. They are met with goodwill and interest. It is a place where work is not a disgrace, even less an honor and where everyone can choose to work, or not – where everyone can go through life according to his own free will. The vagabond is the heroic expression of a strong individuality. There is nothing heroic about having money and not working, but anyone without money who goes through life without gainful employment is a hero.

The Germans however, did resist. Even though it is true that Goethe was the first to clearly accept the English dress, and the most defining characteristic of the young Werther is his attire, which today is used to caricature John Bull. But the Germans are still not convinced. They still express their individuality through odd styles and unusual wardrobe creations and through rather adventurous neckties. Inwardly they are all the same. Each one goes to a production of "Tristan" one day and to a vaudeville show the next, smokes five cigars a day, spouts off well-worn platitudes in the same situations (one need only ask a streetwalker), drinks the same number of beers to encourage drowsiness and, after midnight, starts telling clichéd jokes until he finally slides into bed next to his (hopefully) sleeping wife. Therefore it is necessary for him to show some semblance of individuality through his attire and despises the uniformity of the Englishman.

Who, on the other hand, either drinks himself to death or has never let a drop of alcohol touch his lips.

For some theater – yes, even Shakespeare – is a mortal sin, for others it's the very essence of existence. There are those who, once having succeeded at fatherhood, lose all interest in sexuality, and others – a tendency that could be observed long before de Sade – who are addicted to the vilest of vices. And they all dress the same.

The Englishman goes to buy a necktie: "Give me one for this price and for this occasion and another for this price and this occasion".

The German goes to buy a necktie. But wait, we are getting ahead of ourselves. He first asks all his acquaintances where they bought theirs. He prowls the street for days, looking into shop windows. Finally he takes a friend along to help him choose. He then cheerfully makes his two Mark contribution to the gross national revenue.

However, during the same span of time the Englishman has had a pair of shoes made, or written a poem, or made a fortune on the stock exchange, or made a woman happy, or unhappy.

Let the low-caste *chandala* have his individual trouser cut, the king's son wishes to wander the town without being recognized.

(1908)

Underwear/Undergarments

Recently I had an argument with one of my acquaintances. He accepted the things I had written about the applied arts, but was unhappy with the way I dealt with the fashion and dress issues. He accused me of wanting to standardize the whole world. Where would that leave our wonderful tradition of national costumes?

He began to wax poetic. He reflected on his childhood, on those glorious Sundays in Linz, ruminated about the country folks in their Sunday best, gathering outside the church. What a magnificent, beautiful, picturesque spectacle! And how things had changed! Only the old people still wore their traditional costumes. The young ones were already imitating city dwellers. One would be better advised to try to win the people back to wearing traditional costumes. That should be the task of a journalist concerned with cultural matters!

"So you really like these old costumes?" I interjected. "Of course." "And therefore you wish that these folk costumes are retained for all eternity?" "That is my greatest wish."

Now I had him were I wanted him. "Don't you realize," I said, "what a nasty, selfish person you are? Don't you realize you want to exclude a whole class

ADOLF LOOS

of people, a great class of marvelous people, our peasant farmers, from all the blessings of civilization? And why? To provide some picturesque titillation for your jaded city eye whenever you go out into the country. Why don't *you* go around dressed like that? Aha! Not on your life, eh? But you expect other people to be but figures in a painted landscape, just to satisfy your drunken artist's eye? Why don't *you* go and play the yokel for the councilor of commerce who wants to be thrilled by genuine alpine scenes, and see how you like it. Our peasant farmers have a higher mission to fulfill, than providing an authentic rural human backdrop for summer vacationers. The peasant – the saying is almost a century old – is not a toy."

I have to admit that I like the old costumes very much as well. But that doesn't give me the right to demand that a fellow citizen wear them for my sake. Folk costumes are clothing that have become set in a particular form and have stopped developing. This is always a sign that those who wear them have given up hope of changing their situation. The folk costume is the personification of resignation. It tells us, "I have to give up trying to gain a better position in the struggle for existence. I have to give up the idea of further advancement." When the peasant still went fresh into the fray, filled with the greatest of expectations, he would not have dreamed of wearing the same coat as his grandfather. The rigid clinging to preset styles of dress was unknown throughout the Middle Ages, during the periods of the Peasant Wars, and in the Renaissance. Differences in dress between townsfolk and peasantry were determined by differences in their way of life. During those periods the similarities and differences between townsfolk and peasantry were like those between city dwellers and the farmers of today.

Then the peasant lost his independence. He became a serf, and a serf he had to remain, he and his children's children. What was the point in trying to use his dress to raise himself above his situation, that is, in changing his style of dress? It would make no difference. The peasantry became a caste from which the peasant had no hope of ever escaping. One thing nations divided into castes have in common is this rigid, centuries-long retention of folk costumes.

Then the peasant was emancipated, but only outwardly. Inwardly he still felt inferior to townspeople. They were his lords and masters. The centuries of bondage were still too deeply ingrained within him.

But now a new generation has arrived, a generation that has declared war on folk costumes. In their struggle they have a good ally; the threshing machine. Its arrival in any village means goodbye to all those picturesque hand-me-downs. They are sent where they belong, the costume-dress rental store.

ADOLF LOOS

These are harsh words. But they had to be said. In Austria false sentimentality has even led to the founding of associations whose goal it is to make the peasant keep these symbols of his bondage, when associations with the opposite goal are much more urgently needed. Even the dress we city dwellers wear is far from that worn by the people in the great modern nations. From the outside we look reasonably presentable. In that respect we compare favorably to the rest. If one of the leading Viennese tailors provides us with an outfit, it will certainly be accepted as civilized European attire on the streets of London, New York and Peking. Woe be us should our outer clothing fall off piece-by-piece and we were left standing there in our undergarments! People would realize our European clothes are but a fancy-dress masquerade, for underneath we still wear our national dress.

It is a case of either/or. We must make up our minds. Either we have the courage of our conviction to keep ourselves apart from the rest of humanity and wear our national costume, or we decide we want to be like other people and dress as they do. But to play the modern, advanced European with our outer layers alone, trying to pull the wool over people's eyes with those items of clothing visible to others, is not really the behavior of a gentleman.

While in our outer attire there is a whole world of difference between us and the countryman our underwear is no different than that of the peasant. In Hungary people wear the same under drawers as the *csikos*, the local herdsmen, in Vienna the same as the Lower Austrian peasant. What is it about our underwear that separates us so much from other modern nations?

It is the fact that we are at least fifty years behind the current level England has managed to reach by replacing woven underwear with knitted. In outer clothing there have been no great revolutions in the course of the nineteenth century. All the more far-reaching then, are the undergarment revolutions. A hundred years ago people still wrapped themselves completely in linen. In the course of the last century the hosiery manufacturer has been able, step by step, to recover his market. It happened bit by bit, that is, from one part of the body to another, beginning with the feet and proceeding upward. At the moment knitted hosiery products have conquered the whole of the lower part of English bodies, while the upper part still has to put up with having a linen shirt cover the singlet (undershirt).

It started with the feet. That is where we stand at the moment. We no longer wear foot cloths, we wear stockings. But we still wear linen under drawers, and article that has already become extinct in England and America.

ADOLF LOOS

If a man from the Balkans, where they still wear foot cloths, were to come to Vienna and go to an undergarment shop to purchase his accustomed hosiery, he would be astounded to hear the shop assistant tell him that no shop in the city stocked foot cloths, though he could order some.

"But what do people here wear on their feet, then?" the visitor would ask.

"Socks."

"Socks?" They are very uncomfortable – and too hot in summer. Doesn't anyone wear foot cloths any more?"

"Oh yes, very old people. But younger people find foot cloths uncomfortable."

Our man from the Balkans decides with a heavy heart to give socks a try, and thus moves up one step on the ladder of civilization.

Plovdiv (Bulgaria) is to Vienna as Vienna is to New York. Let us imagine we go there to try to buy not footcloths – they wouldn't even know what we are talking about – but linen drawers. I kindly must ask you to reread the dialogue above, replacing "man from the Balkans" with "man from Vienna", and "foot cloths" with "linen drawers". For that would be exactly how it would go. I speak from personal experience; in fact, that was how the dialogue transpired when I was in America. I just put in foot cloths to in order to adapt to Viennese conditions.

Those who find woven materials more comfortable than knitted ones are welcome to wear them. It would be nonsense to impose on people a cultural form that went against their inner feeling. The fact is, people who are culturally up-to-date find linen uncomfortable. We will, therefore, just have to wait until the Austrians also begin to find it uncomfortable. The increasing popularity of physical exercise, of sports, which emanates from England, is another factor contributing to this aversion to linen underwear. Starched collars, cuffs and dickeys (false shirtfronts) are also a hindrance to sporting activity. The un-starched shirtfront is the harbinger of the un-starched collar, and the function of both is to prepare the way for jersey and flannel undershirts.

There is, however, one great danger in a jersey undergarment. It really is only meant for people who enjoy washing. Many Germans see jersey underwear as an excuse not to wash at all. It is after all, from Germany that all inventions designed to avert washing come. Germany gave us celluloid collars, cuffs, dickeys and ties with attached shirtfronts out of the same material. Germany also gave us the doctrine that washing is harmful to one's health, and that one can wear a jersey undershirt for years – for as long as those around do not raise serious objections. Americans cannot imagine a German without a dazzling white, but false, shirtfront. This can be seen frequently in the German caricatures found in American humor magazines. You can recognize a German by the tip of his false dickey sticking out from under his vest. According to American caricaturists there is only one other class of person who wears a false shirtfront, the tramp and the hobo.

The false shirtfront is truly no symbol for claiming that cleanliness is next to godliness. It is all the more unfortunate, then, that this sorry indicator of the cultural level of a nation can be seen in that section of the exhibition where our best tailors have their displays. That reduces the standard of an otherwise elegant exhibit quite a bit.

A completely new type of shop has been introduced: *tailors and outfitters*. An *outfitter* keeps everything in stock belonging to menswear. Not an easy task. For every article he sells he takes the responsibility for the appropriate *distinguished* look of the buyer. In a well-run gentleman's *outfitter* one can expect to be able to choose an item completely at random and not end up with something not in good taste, i.e. not correct. A true gentleman's *outfitter* cannot make any concessions to the needs of the masses. The excuse that one has to cater to all tastes should never cross the lips of a leading *outfitter*. Errors of judgment should be unthinkable, and if one should happen to occur, it is his duty toward his customers to remove the offending article from his premises immediately. Most certainly, not an easy task. It is difficult enough for him to attain the leading position in the field of men's fashion, yet it is even more difficult to retain it. Only a tiny proportion of his stock is made in his own workshop. He is principally a dealer. His relationship with craftsmen is similar to that of a collector, or the director of an art gallery with his artists. They too have a duty to select the best from among the wealth of objects that latter have created. This is enough of a task to fully occupy the mind and soul of any person.

There is something that needs to be said in regard to the flood of anonymous letters I receive, usually expressing the "suspicion," that someone on whom I have commented favorably does not make his goods himself. Even if I thought that were significant, I could not attempt to establish the provenance of the goods. I am not a detective. It is of complete indifference to me where they were made. The important point is that the outfitter can supply these wares in the proper quality. Whether he has his own workshop, or commissions other craftsmen to do the work, has no bearing on the quality of the articles, and that is what I am commenting on.

The exhibition of the knitted-goods manufacturers also contains some excellent items. But one will search in vain for white knitted underwear, the only correct kind. It is well-known that, at the moment, our ladies are wearing white or bluish-white stockings, or is that something still to come in Vienna?

It is sad to see so many ready-made neckties among the numerous exhibitors of ladies' fashions. Even on a man these look rather vulgar. A tie consisting of a knot or a bow in a piece of elastic around the neck is on a par with paper underwear and paste jewelry. And not to mention those neck cloths which attempt to achieve the splendid effect of a cravat wound twice around the neck by means of a piece of cardboard covered in silk and few other "patents", the favored neckwear of our provincial dandy. That our Viennese girls and women are using such substitutes instead of wearing properly tied bows show that the oft-praised Viennese chic is dying out. I wish there were a shop in Vienna where the owner can proudly tell anyone who asks for a ready-made tie, "Ready-made ties? No! We do not stock such items."

(1898?)

Men's Fashion

Ah, to be well dressed, who does not desire to be well dressed? In our century we have managed to abolish the dress code and hence, it is the right of everyman to dress like a king. In order to discern the cultural standing of a nation one could actually employ as a guideline the fact of how many of its inhabitants actually make use of this libertine achievement – In England and the United States everyone, in the Balkan countries only the upper class. In Austria? I do dare not to answer this question?

An American philosopher once stated: A young man can count himself rich when he has a brain in his head and a good suit in his closet. This man knows what he was talking about. He obviously knows something about people. What is the value of all common sense if you cannot reveal it through your attire? The English and the Americans expect everyone to be well dressed.

The Germans go a step further. They want to be well dressed as well. Should the English wear wide trousers they immediately attempt to prove – I am not sure exactly how, perhaps with the help of the aesthetic principals of old Fredrich Theodor Vischer[1] or of the golden mean – that this is unaesthetic and

---

1 Frederich Theodor Vischer was a German writer on the philosophy of art.

ADOLF LOOS

only narrow trousers can truly be considered elegant. Amidst bluster, rants and cursing they let their pants become wider year after year, while bemoaning that *Fashion is a tyrant*. But what is this really all about? Has a reassessment of values taken place? In the meantime, the English again are wearing tighter trousers, and once again the same methods are employed to prove the aesthetics regarding the elegance of trousers once again. Does this make sense?

The English can only laugh at the German obsession for beauty in fashion. The Medici Venus, the Pantheon, a painting by Botticelli, a song by Burns; yes, they are beautiful – but a pair of trousers?! Or whether a jacket has three or four buttons? Or whether a waistcoat is cut high or low? When I hear people discussing the beauty of such things I just don't know what to say. I become nervous, when I am asked somewhat mischievously about an article of clothing: "Isn't that lovely"?

Germans from the upper class are quite similar to the English. They are happy when they are well dressed. Beauty is not part of the equation. The great poets, great painters and great architects dress appropriately. The pretentious poets, painters and architects present their bodies as an altar on which satin collars, aesthetic trouser materials, *Art Nouveau* neckties are to be sacrificed for the sake of beauty.

Well dressed, what does that actually mean? It means to be correctly dressed.

Correctly dressed! It is as if with these words I have revealed a secret that up till now has cloaked our perception of fashion. Words like lovely, chic, elegant, fetching and snappy are but vain attempts to provide explanatory terms for fashion. But this is not at all the point. It is all about being dressed in an inconspicuous manner. A red tailcoat stands out in a ballroom. Therefore red tails are not fashionable in a ballroom. A top hat stands out on the ice rink, therefore it is unfashionable to wear while ice-skating. Anything conspicuous in high society is considered crude.

This basic principal, however cannot be applied everywhere. A coat that hardly would be noticed in Hyde Park could certainly be conspicuous in Peking, in Zanzibar, and in front of St. Stephens Cathedral in Vienna. It looks very European. One simply cannot expect a person from a culturally advanced society to dress Chinese in China, African in Zanzibar and Viennese in Vienna! Therefore the previous statement needs to be qualified: in order to be well-dressed one should not be conspicuous within the center of one's own culture.

Currently the center of Western culture is London. As London is quite large, it could quite well be the case that, during a walk, one could find oneself in areas where one would appear to be quite conspicuous. Strictly speaking, one would have to change one's coat from street to street. This is impossible.

Now that we have established the basic premise and considered all eventualities we can formulate the following conclusion: an article of clothing is modern, when it is possible to wear it in one's native cultural environment at a certain occasion in the best society and it does not attract any unwarranted attention.

This English point of view, which should make perfect sense to any cultivated person, encounters strong resistance among the middle and lower class Germans. No nation has so many dandies as the Germans. A dandy is a person for whom clothes serve only one purpose: to stand out from the crowd. The arguments used to justify this zany behavior vary from the ethical to hygienic to the aesthetic. From the master himself, Karl Wilhelm Diefenbach[2] to Professor Jäger[3], from the "modern" poetasters to the pampered son of a Viennese landlord there is a common spiritual bond uniting them. Yet, despite this bond they do not get along. No dandy will ever admit to being one. A dandy will always make fun of the other and, under the pretense or getting rid of dandyism, continues to commit new dandyisms. The contemporary dandy or the dandy per se is only one form of a globally widely ramified species.

---

2 Karl Wilhelm Diefenbach was a German painter and a leading advocate of a "natural" way of life.

3 Gustav Jäger advocated clothing reform. He objected to vegetable fibers in clothes and created a woolen material known in English as "Jaeger".

It is these dandies that Germans believe set the fashion trends. It is an honor that these harmless creates do not deserve. From the aforementioned it is quite evident that the dandy's sense of fashion is not even modern. That would not be of any use to him anyway. The dandy wears that, what those around him *think* is modern.

But, isn't that actually the same as modern? Not at all. This is the reason the dandies are different in every city. What makes an impression in city A, has already lost its appeal in city B. Someone who is admired in Berlin could be in danger of being laughed of the street in Vienna. In the best circles, however, where it is considered rather petty to be concerned with such matters, the preferred changes in fashion are those least likely to be noticed by the middle classes. The elite no longer enjoy the protection of sumptuary laws, and the idea of being copied the very next day by everyone and anyone is not an idea that appeals to them. Should that be the case, one would immediately have to find a replacement. In order to avoid this perpetual hunt for new materials and styles, they insist on the greatest discretion. Each year the new style is an open secret, carefully guarded by the best tailors, until one day it is revealed by some fashion journal. But even then it takes a few years before the last man in the country hears about it. And only now does the dandy come into play, and adds his take on things. However, through this extended process the original style has undergone substantial change, dependent on, among other things, geographical locations.

The best tailors throughout the world, the ones capable of outfitting someone according to the principals of true elegance, can be counted on the fingers of two hands. There are some great metropolises in the old world with millions of inhabitants who simply do not have such a unique tailor. Even in Berlin there was none to be found until a Viennese master craftsman, E. Ebenstein, opened a store there. Before Ebenstein's arrival the Berlin Court was forced to have a great portion of its wardrobe made by Poole's of London. That we have several of the leading names in Vienna is only due to the lucky happenstance that many members of our aristocracy are frequent guests in the *drawing room* of the Queen and have much of their wardrobe made in England. This distinguished style they then brought to Vienna, which in turn brought the Viennese tailors an enviable international reputation. It is probably true to ascertain that the Viennese High Society is better dressed than any other on the European continent, since the standards of all the tailors have been raised by the leading firms.

The leading houses and those just below them all have one thing in common: a fear of publicity. Wherever possible they attempt to keep the clientele small.

They might not be quite as exclusive as some of the more noted London houses, which open their doors for you only if the Prince of Wales has recommended you to them. However any form of exterior pomposity is frowned upon. It took a great deal of persuasion by the Exhibition Committee to convince a few of the best tailors in Vienna to exhibit their collections. One must admire the way they managed to circumvent the situation by only exhibiting the pieces that were impossible to copy. The most adroit was Ebenstein. He exhibited a "tuxedo" (incorrectly termed a Smoking) ideal for the tropics (!) a "hunting vest", a lady's uniform for the colonel-in-chief of a Prussian regiment and a "coaching coat" with engraved mother of pearl buttons; each of which is a work of art in itself. A. Keller brought a *frock coat* with the obligatory grey trousers, in which one could quite comfortably travel to London, as well as some extraordinary uniforms. Their "Norfolk Jacket" also appears to be very well made. Uzel and Son exhibit the specialty of their shop: court and state uniforms. They must be good otherwise the company would not be able to maintain its leading position in this field for so long. Franz Bubacek has brought samples of sports attire for the Emperor to the exhibition. The cut of their Norfolk Jacket is both new and correct. Mr. Bubacek has shown great courage in his choices for the exhibit. He clearly is not afraid of imitators, copycats. The

ADOLF LOOS

same can be said about Goldman & Salatsch who have brought their most noted line: uniforms of the "yacht squadron". Joseph Scalley are exhibiting a lavish collection of uniforms, all showing the precision stitching this company is known for. Emerich Schönbrunn perhaps provides a transition. Some items prove that they can produce work of the most refined taste, yet they also show that they are quite prepared to make concessions to other circles.

This however, brings me to the end of my unconditional praise. The overall exhibition of the Association of Vienna Tailors does not deserve it. In dealing with individual customers one must often turn a blind eye as the clients', insisting that their personal wishes are respected, are frequently responsible for some of the poor taste. Here the tailors could have shown how far above their customers in matters of taste that they are *well able to compete with the* leading companies when they have a free hand. Most, however let this opportunity slip away. This was evident in their rather ignorant choice of material. They made Paletots (light overcoats) out of *covert coat* material and used Paletot material to make *covert coats*. Lounge suits were made out of Norfolk jacket material and patterned material was used to make a frock coat.

The cuts were not much better. Few held the viewpoint that it was their task to create a refined piece, and most catered to the dandies. And there they can wallow in their double-breasted vests, checkered suits and velvet collars to their heart's content. One company went so far as to put blue velvet cuffs on a jacket! Certainly, the next fashion trend...

I will mention a few houses that have kept themselves somewhat distant from this fashion inferno. Anton Adam are good, but their vests are cut too low. Alois Decker also deserves mention. Alexander Deutsch show a good winter overcoat, Joseph Hummel a good Ulster and a Norfolk jacket, P. Kroupa derogate their otherwise very correct frock coat with a braid. Emanuel Kuhl are distinguished, as are Leopold Kurzweil. Johann Neidl and Wenzel Slaby, each presented a correct suit with a frock coat and Joseph Rosiwall have a good dress suit on display. I would have liked to mention another company that exhibited its wares as well, but as I attempted to lift the pleat on their Norfolk jacket, the purpose that is to allow the arm freedom of movement, I could not. It was a fake pleat.

(1898?)

ADOLF LOOS

(Gentle)Men's Hats

How is fashion created? Who creates fashion? These are surely very difficult questions.

It was left to the Viennese Association for Hat Fashion to easily find solutions for these questions – at least when it comes to headwear. The aforementioned group meets twice a year and, sitting around a green table, decrees the form of hat that shall be worn the following season – around the globe. Around the globe – that is what must be borne in mind. They are not creating something for a Viennese folk costume, something that would immediately be taken up by petty thieves, buggy drivers, pimps, dandies and other local Viennese types. Oh no! That is not the reason that the members of the Hat Fashion Association rack their brains. The fashion trend is created solely for the gentleman. As the attire of such has absolutely nothing in common with the various local traditional costumes, unless it is related to a local sports' activity, and the gentlemen of the world all adhere to the same dress norm, it is quite evident that the Viennese Hat Fashion Association sets the tone for all men's headwear in the civilized Western World.

Who would have thought that the solutions to these questions would be so simple? I now view the honest hat maker with great reverence for he, with his vote for the further increase in the height of the silk hat, is able to provide the necessary majority of one vote to ensure that this *fashion measure* passes. He has forced all the male *pavement-pounders* from Paris to Yokohama to wear even taller top hats next year if they still wish still to be considered part of the high society. But what do those from Paris to Yokohama know! What do they know about the honest hat maker from the 11th District in Vienna! They might jabber something about the tyranny of fashion or, at best, something about that capricious Goddess of Fashion. If they only knew! Our honest hat maker in the 11th District is the tyrant, the god of fashion!

It is would be almost inconceivable to image what the consequences might have been if this man would have been hindered from participating in this fashion vote: be it through a cold, his stern wife not letting him go out that evening, or even, that it just completely slipped his mind. Then the whole world would be condemned to wearing a lower top hat. But one can hope that the members of the hat fashion association, fully aware of their colossal responsibility to the world, will not let anything deter them from casting their vote twice a year.

I think I can image the question my readers might now have: is it possible that the hat makers from Paris, London, New York and Bombay will let hat fashion be dictated by the Viennese hat makers?

ADOLF LOOS

Sheepishly, despite all I have said, I must respond with: sadly no. These bad people, with "perfidious Albion" at the vanguard, are not at all concerned about the results of this vote. Well, are these vote results then without merit? To tell the truth, yes. These elections are but a harmless game, just as harmless as if held by the Budapest or Chicago hat makers. The hat shape of the distinguished gentleman, who wishes his hat to be considered distinguished around the world, will not be affected by any of this.

But wait, this game is not as harmless as it appears. There are more men of taste than our hat makers generally assume, and they certainly do not want to wear hats whose acceptability ends with the black yellow marks of the Austrian border. But, this is precisely the kind of hat our hat makers are producing according to the resolution of the hat makers association. As a consequence these distinguished gentlemen are compelled to purchase English hats. Every year we can see how English hats are becoming increasingly more prevalent, despite the fact that they are of the same quality, but almost 100 percent more expensive, while the type dictated by the Hat Fashion Association is becoming more removed from those preferred by the best society. This development makes one even sadder if one takes into consideration that, with our excellent felt and reasonable prices, we are more than capable of competing with anyone in the world. The success of the Viennese hat in other countries continually fails because of its incorrect shape and style.

Among their customers in fashionable society, our leading companies had extremely disappointing experiences with the models of the Hat Fashion Association, and quickly gave up their allegiance to that organization. You will not find their models at Pless or Habig. Their liberation from the Association's guidelines made itself felt in exports. Now you can find Habig hats all over the world, in New York as well as in Rio de Janeiro.

I however, fail to see why the Court hat maker, with all his foreign connections and, thanks to his distinguished clientele can stock the correct models, should be offering different hats than the provincial master hat maker.

Instead of proclaiming as modern some hat, a concoction that has sprung from the imagination of one of its members, what the Hat Fashion Association instead should be doing is publicizing the model accepted as modern throughout the world. Above all, what the most distinguished circles consider modern. This would result in an increase in exports and a decrease in imports. After all it certainly would be no disaster if everyone, even in the smallest provincial village, were to wear a hat as elegant as the Viennese aristocrat. The age of sumptuary laws is past. As things are, however, some of the decisions of this association are harming our hat-making industry. At the moment top hats are being worn a bit lower than in the previous season. The association, on the other hand, has decreed a further increase in height of the top hat for the coming winter. And the result? English hat makers are already preparing for massive exports of silk hats to the Austrian market, as the modern style will not be available at every Viennese hat makers.

There are other aspects in which the association's activities could be beneficial to the industry. Our Austrian national hat, the loden hat, is just beginning a journey that could take it right around the globe. It has already reached England. The Prince of Wales came to know and appreciate its qualities during his hunting trips to Austria and took it home with him, where it quickly won over English society – ladies as well as gentlemen. It is indeed a critical time, then, especially for the manufacturers of loden hats. The question is, you see, who is going to make the loden hats for the English society? The Austrians, surely? At least as long as we can produce the styles English society wants. But that requires infinite discernment, precise knowledge of society, sensitivity in questions of taste, and a good nose for future trends. One cannot dictate style to that kind of client, simply by a crude majority vote. I assume the large manufacturers are well aware of this, but I think small hat makers should also profit from the advantageous association that has arisen for their products. It is for them that the hat association should pursue the matter, if it feels it is up to the task. Perhaps even the large manufacturers are not aware of the situation. In that case the fortunate English will inherit the treasure that small hat makers in alpine regions have carefully guarded for a thousand years.

The point is the English manufacturer conducts his business in a different way than his Austrian counterpart. Different hats are produced for different markets. We should not be under any delusions. The English hat we buy in Vienna is a compromise between the modern hat and the hat recommended by the Viennese Hat Fashion Association. Even for primitive nations they produce items that are popular there and, as you can see, treat us the same way as they do savages. And they are right in doing so. In that way they sell a large number of hats to us, for they would do poor business with the modern hat, the hat worn in the best circles of society. They do not sell the Viennese the hat that is modern, but rather the hat the Viennese *think* is modern. And that is certainly quite a difference.

The correct hat is sold only in London. When I was running out of London hats I went around to the shops here in search of the *correct shape*. That was when I discovered the English hats sold here do not correspond to the ones sold in London. I asked one hat maker to order a hat for me from England in the same style as worn by the members of the British royal family. Expense was of no object, but a written guarantee from the London house was. I got nowhere. After months of excuses, after a considerable sum had been wasted on telegrams, the English company broke off negotiations. It would be easy for the hat makers association to obtain these hat forms. It is not a matter of speed either. We would be quite content to be able to buy today the hat English society was wearing three years ago. For us that would be such a hyper-modern hat that no one in Vienna would notice the difference. That is what one can expect of a modern hat. Fashion progresses more slowly, slower than one might think. Objects that are really modern stay so for a long time. If one hears of an item of clothing that is out of date the very next season then one can be sure it was never truly modern, but only falsely professed to being such.

Looking at our hat makers' display in the Rotunda, it is heartbreaking to think such a capable industry no longer has a share in the export trade. Apart from the Emperor's portrait on the lining, there are no examples of bad taste at all, and even the smallest master craftsman is capable of producing hats of the same excellent quality as the leading houses. The same cannot be said of other branches of the clothing industry, and that shows one how high the standards of our hat makers are. Each one strives to impress through the obvious inherent competence, and all of them refuse to employ the usual exhibition trick of attracting the public's attention by creating outlandish styles. The result is that throughout this section of the exhibit the tone is one of restraint and refinement. The Hat Makers Association has brought together in one display the work of twelve hatters, large and small companies, all of excellent quality. What makes our Court hat makers – Habig, Berger, Ita, and Skrivan – stand out is the rich variety of items they have on display. Unfortunately I cannot judge the correctness of the shapes, since I have been in Vienna for more than two years now. As far as the elegance of the trimmings is concerned, I would award the prize to Ita.

It is to be hoped our Hat Makers Fashion Association will make every attempt to catch up with other civilized countries. An Austrian national fashion is a figment of the imagination, and to insist on trying to create one would cause incalculable damage to our industry. China is starting to tear down its walls, and it is right to do so. Let us not allow people, out of a false sense of patriotism, to erect a great wall here, cutting us off from other nations.

(1898)

ADOLF LOOS

Footwear/Shoes

Tempora mutantur, nos et matamur in illis. Times change, and we change with them. Our feet change as well. Soon they will be small, or large, narrow, or broad. And the shoes made by the shoemakers will be small, or large, or narrow, or broad.

Of course, it's not quite that simple. The shape of our feet does not change from season to season. This takes centuries or, at least a generation. It just isn't possible to turn a large foot into a small foot on a fashion whim. In that respect the creative makers of other fashion items have it easier. Full waist, wasp waist, high shoulders, sloping shoulders; these and many other styles can be attained by the aid of a new line, a bit of padding, or something similar. However, shoemakers have to stick to the shape of the individual foot. If they want to (re)introduce small shoes, they have to wait patiently until the "Big Foot" dynasty has died out.

But it is evident that not all people have the same foot shape at the same time. People who make greater use of their feet will develop larger ones; people who use them less will have smaller ones. What can the shoemaker do about this? What shape of foot should he use as his standard – for he must endeavor to produce a contemporary product. He too, wants to get ahead in a competitive world and therefore wishes to make his products as marketable as possible.

Consequently, he does what all the other crafts-men do. He bases his designs on the shape of the foot of the socially most prominent class. In the Middle Ages the knights were socially dominant, riders who, because they spent a great amount of time on horse-back had smaller feet then the common foot-folk. This in turn meant that the small foot was modern, and by lengthening it with the turned up toe the craftsman was able to emphasize its slimness, which was regarded as the most desirable feature at the time. With the decline of Knighthood, the pedestrian burgher replaced the knight in the social standing and the large, broad foot of the patrician with his relaxed way of walking became fashionable. During the seventeenth and eighteenth centuries the pre-dominance of the royal courts meant that walking was on the decline again, and the widespread use of the sedan chair led to the ascendancy of small shoes with high heels, ideal for the park and the palace, but not suitable for the street.

The revival of Germanic culture brought horse-back riding back to prominence. In the eighteenth century everyone who wanted to be fashionable wore English riding boots, even if they did not own a horse. The riding boot was the symbol of a free man, a man who had finally liberated himself from the confines of buckled shoes, gleaming parquet floors and the oppressive air of the courts. Feet remained small, but the high heels, of no use to horsemen, disappeared. Throughout the century that followed, our century that is, people endeavored to have as small a foot as possible.

But in the course of this century the human foot has undergone a transformation. Changing social conditions have meant that year after year we walk more and more quickly. Saving time, means saving money. Even the best circles – that is, people who actually have time to spare – have been caught up in this change and increased their pace. Nowadays the normal pace of an agile and active person can be compared to that of running footmen preceding a carriage in the previous century. Walking as slowly as people did in earlier times would be impossible for us today. Life is just too hectic. In the eighteenth century soldiers marched at a pace that, to us, would seem like standing still on each leg alternately and be most tiring. The increase in walking speed can best be illustrated by the fact that the army of Frederick the Great was 70 paces per minute, while the modern army takes 120. (Our parade regulations specify 115 to 117 paces per minute, but it is very difficult to keep contemporary soldiers to that, as they tend to increase the speed on their own accord. A new edition of the regulations will have to take this modern development into account – something that certainly will not harm the overall tactical readiness of the army.) Using this as a basis, it is quite possible to extrapolate how many paces per minute – or all people who wish to get somewhere quickly – will be marching in a hundred years from now.

People of more advanced civilizations walk at a faster pace than those who are behind the times – the Americans walk more quickly than the Italians for example. In New York you always have the feeling there must have been an accident somewhere. And a Viennese of the eighteenth century walking on the Kärntnerstrasse of today would have the impression that something has happened.

Therefore it is evident that we now walk at a faster pace. This means that we push off from the ground more strongly with our big toe. And, indeed, our big toes are becoming bigger and stronger. Strolling at a leisurely pace results in a broadening of the foot, while fast walking, through the more extensive use of the middle foot, invariably leads to a lengthening. As the other toes, in particular the little toe, cannot keep pace with this development, they atrophy through reduction of use, which in turn results in a narrowing of the foot.

The pedestrian has, so to speak, overtaken then horseback rider. The pedestrian is simply a further development of the German ethnic principal: To get ahead on one's own will be the motto for the next century. The horse was merely a transitional phase between the sedan bearer and one's own self. The story of the nineteenth century is also the story of the glory as well as the demise of the horse tradition. The smell of the stables was the most noble of perfumes and horse racing our national pastime. The horseman was the spoiled favorite of the German folksong: A Riders End, The Rider's Lady, and The Horseman's Farewell. The pedestrian was non-existent. The entire world dressed like a horseman. When we wanted to dress up for a special occasion, we put on our riding coat, the tailcoat. Every student had his mount and the streets where filled with riders of all sorts.

How things have changed! The horseman is the man of the plains, of the flat lands. The English country gentlemen bred horses and appeared at the *hunt* from time to time to jump the fences chasing after the fox. He has been replaced by a man who lives in the mountains, who finds pleasure in climbing to the peaks and risking his life to take himself above the habitations of man, the highlander, the Scot.

The rider wears high boots and long narrow trousers that come down over the knee and end in a very narrow leg (*riding breeches*). They are of no use to the pedestrian or the mountain climber. Whether in Scotland or the Alps, he wears lace-up shoes and long stockings that should not come above the knees, but leave them free. The Scot wears his well-known kilt, the alpine mountaineer leather shorts, *Lederhosen*, but in principle they are the same. There is a difference between the plainsman and the mountaineer in the type of material used: the former wears fine cloth, the latter coarse weaves (*home spun* and loden).

Mountain climbing has become national sport. The very same people who a hundred years ago had such a profound dread of high mountains are fleeing the flatlands and making off toward higher ground. Mountain climbing, using one's own physical strength to push higher and higher, is currently considered one of the noblest of passions. But, must those who do not live in the mountains be excluded from this noble passion? One must only remember that in the previous century horse riding was called a "noble passion". A means was sought that would allow these people in the low country (as well?) to exercise themselves in a similar way. Therefore the bicycle was invented.

The cyclist is the mountaineer of the plains. Therefore he dresses similarly. High boots and riding breeches are of no use to him. He wears trousers that are wide at the knee, closing below it in a turn-up, around which the turned down tops of the stockings fit (The stockings are turned over at the top both in the Alps and in Scotland, so they stay up.) In this way the knee has room to move under the trousers and can bend and stretch without restriction. By the way, it is worth mentioning that there are some people in Vienna who apparently do not know the real purpose of turn-ups as they tuck their stockings in under the turn-ups. They leave just as silly an impression as the various city tourists in alpine garb who infest the Alps in the summer. Like the mountaineer, the cyclist wears lace-up shoes.

Laced shoes will dominate the next century just as riding boots have done in this century. The English have already made a direct transition and wear both styles today. We, however, have created a hideous hybrid for this transitional period: the elastic-sided boot. The ugliness of the elastic-sided boot became immediately apparent with the advent of short trousers. It quickly became evident that elastic-sided boots could not be worn without the charity of a concealing long trouser leg. Our officers used to wear gaiters to conceal them, and were justifiably unhappy when uniform regulations were more strictly applied and the infantry was forbidden to wear gaiters. For us, elastic-sided boots are dead, as dead as the tailcoat during daylight hours, the comic effect of which can only be appreciated when we go for a walk with it in the street. Even in sweltering heat we have to put on an overcoat to cover up, or take a cab. Producing a comic effect: that has been the death knell for any item of clothing.

As a result of their various pedestrian activities, the foot of our upper crust is no longer as small as it used to be. They are getting bigger and bigger. The Englishman's and the Englishwoman's big feet no longer incur the mockery that they used to. We climb mountains as well, ride bicycles and – *horribile dictu* – are developing "English" feet. But, this is hardly a disturbing process. The small foot is slowly beginning to lose its attraction, especially in a man. I recently was sent a description of Rigo from America. One of his acquaintances begins: "I knew the gypsy," and in the course of the description that follows states: "A pair of disgustingly small feet were peering out from under his trousers". Disgustingly small feet! It sounds convincing, this new doctrine from America: disgustingly small feet. Poor Saint Heinrich Clauren[1], if you heard that, you whose heroes could never have had feet small enough, on which in noble virility they danced into the dreams of a hundred thousand German maidens. Tempora mutantur...

Button shoes, which are acceptable only in patent leather, should be mentioned here as well. They are shoes for leisure. Were patent leather shoes are required, such as with full-dress uniforms, the Eng-

---

1 Pseudonym of Karl Gottlieb Samuel Heun (1771–1854) a purveyor of sentimental and mildly titillating fiction to the German middle classes.

ADOLF LOOS

lish as well as their aristocratic regiment wear patent leather boots with polished legs under their trousers. The only acceptable dancing shoes are patent leather, (*pumps*).

I will deal with Viennese shoemakers and the Viennese pedestrian in a separate chapter.

(1904?)

Shoemakers

When this journal published a reply to the article on the activities of the Vienna Association of Hat Fashion, we could not imagine the significance of the step we were taking. And know we have to live with the consequences. The whole industry has been struck by an epidemic of retraction mania. Everyone with a different opinion expects, as a matter of course, to see his views appear in print. "Setting the record straight" has become a national sport. Thus a Herr S., who has been "active in the shoemaking business for twenty years!" as he assures us, emphasized by the exclamation mark following his signature, "permits himself to request the inclusion of following corrections, followed by a whole series of paragraphs beginning with, "It's wrong to…"

Perhaps our readers will be curious to know what Herr S. feels is necessary to correct. Let us take a few points at random. "It is wrong," says Herr S., "to compare mountaineering to bicycling." Or, "It is wrong to say that every student has a mount." Or, "It is wrong to say that laced shoes will dominate the next century." Another gentleman, a Herr Sch., has also requested the inclusion of a few of his lines, hoping to make a contribution to the improvement of the currently depressed Austrian shoemaking industry.

He however suffers under a gross misconception. He has taken my enthusiastic description of the Vienna Association of Hat Fashion at face value. He vigorously takes exception to the view that activities such as mountaineering, walking, and cycling have led to the widespread acceptance of laced shoes, continuing, "We must, therefore, search for other reasons. I am referring to the light footwear that led to the widespread adoption of laced shoes; the shoemakers promoted laced shoes and brought out appealing models. And there we have it. It's the shoemaker who creates the fashion. Herr Loos recently told us a delightful story about how the Hat Fashion Association dictates the trend, and here we have the same situation."

Now, it is not possible that everyone who requests inclusion can be included. Unintentional humor is always amusing, but this is not a comic magazine. The original reader's letter defending the activities of the Hat Fashion Association was an interesting addition to my attacks and did much to clear up the situation. It was more powerful than my own arguments, more devastating than my criticism and must surely put an end to the system of voting on next season's designs. More powerful and more devastating because it comes from the Association's own camp. The public began to wonder, and rightly so, what the good taste of these people who dictate it upon others is really all about. That there are people who consider the models recommended by the Hat Fashion Association elegant enough was never in dispute. But what kind of people are they? What about their taste? Herr Kessler's letter provided a clear answer to that. To have his Majesty's portrait printed on the lining is compatible to *his* taste. To back up his argument, he refers to Bukovina[1], where they make similar use of the portraits of the nation's leaders. Now the public knows where it stands. On the one hand England, on the other, Bukovina!

The letters from the gentlemen of the shoemaking industry, on the other hand, do nothing to clear up the situation. Basically they all say the same thing, namely, that the introduction of the laced shoe has damaged the Austrian shoe manufacturers, since it has displaced the elastic-sided boot, which, strangely enough, they consider Austria's national shoe. This accusation is, of course, completely unfounded. Shoes and boots will always be bought, and whether they are made according to this system or that is of no relevance to the shoemaker. This is not the case for the manufacturer of elastic, who will now have to look to other products. The wheels of time take their toll, and a million tons of printer's ink will not bring back the elastic-sided boot.

---

1 A small and backward monarchy on the eastern edge of the Austrian Empire, now a part of the Ukraine.

ADOLF LOOS

This is demonstrated by the Exhibition itself. Out of the 192 shoes of the Shoemakers' Cooperative on display there are only nine elastic-sided boots, three for the ladies, three for the gentlemen and three for uniformed officers. The message of these statistics is unequivocal. And in ten years' time? It is not hard to predict that the last nine will have disappeared as well.

After the English, our shoemakers surely make the best shoes in the world. There are excellent shoe-makers to be found in all European capitals, but the consistent craftsmanship of the average shoemaker puts Austria above all other countries as far as foot-wear is concerned. This is all the more surprising as our shoemakers are poorly paid for their work. The public is increasingly forcing prices down, and the difference, if the tradesman does not want to go out of business, is made up in the shoes themselves. Do not believe that the shoemaker derives any pleasure out of it, but you are forcing him to do substandard work. He dreams of the best leather, the best work-manship. How he would love to spend one more day on a pair shoes. How he hates forcing his assistants to work faster, well aware of the fact that it means he will have to ignore a certain amount of shoddy work-manship. But life knows no mercy; it will not do him that favor. He must, must, *and must* make those shoes at that price. So he decides, with a heavy heart to fire his good but slow assistant and to scrimp and save on the raw materials. Even starting with the thread? But it is you, the customer who takes a special pleasure in forcing your shoemaker to lower his prices once again by one *krone, a krone* you are quite happy to spend on a better seat in the theater if your usual ones are sold out, you are our craftsman's worst enemy. Bargaining and haggling and pushing down prices have a demoralizing effect on both producer and consumer.

And despite all this they still are such good shoes. Our shoemakers happen to be competent men – contemplative men, full of individuality. It is no coincidence that the greatest poet and the greatest philosopher to come from our craftsmen were both shoemakers. And how many Hans Saches and Jakob Boehmes have sat – and are perhaps still are sitting – on the cobblers stool who have had the same creative spirit, but never wrote anything down? Perhaps the reason the Germans have such good cobblers and such good soldiers is that every capable, individual, and therefore, in their parents' opinion, naughty boy is continually admonished: "If you don't do as you're told you will end up as a shoemaker's apprentice or at the military academy". Sometimes this is actually the case.

Our shoe *wearers* deserve much less praise. Early on in this article I mentioned that shoemakers must base their styles on the shape of foot of the socially dominant class. They are the ones the shoes must fit. But people who do not have the same shape of foot still demand the same models from their shoemakers. The consequences are all those deformed feet you only see among people who do not belong to the dominant class. And it is the shoemaker who is blamed for their vanity. The low price does not allow him to make an individual shoe for his customer, which means that even if an old last can be adapted with a template, it will not give the correct balance, which is essential for an even tread. This balance, one of the most difficult tasks in shoemaking, is not determined by the shape of the sole alone but to a large extent by the gait and the habits of the wearer.

Shoemakers who make expensive shoes unfortunately earn less from them than those whose deliberate policy is to supply a mediocre product. Let me cite two examples: the eighteen-*gulden* shoemaker and the six-*gulden* shoemaker. The former makes a shoe last which, including his own time costs him six *gulden*, has the uppers made by an assistant whom, because of his excellent workmanship, he pays three *gulden* per day and spends three *gulden* on the material for the uppers. The six-*gulden* shoemaker uses an old last and ready made uppers at about two *gulden* per pair from the factory. Therefore the former invests sixty-six percent of the price for materials and labor, the latter only thirty-three percent. In addition, too little is done to care for and preserve footwear. Most people scrimp on the purchase of good wood and thus wear out their shoes more quickly than people who keep them on shoe-trees overnight.

After the banning of "immoral" shoes, the exhibition has nothing but good, solid footwear on display. It is regrettable that shoes, whose sole purpose it was to attract people's attention, needed to be declared "immoral" to keep them out of the exhibition. How much more dignified it would have been for the whole industry if such shoes had been rejected from the outset because of their impracticality as footwear. Shoemakers who practice such slick self-advertising cannot seriously expect us to believe these boots could be worn to learn the *tiptoe* dance. This is impertinence, and even people who know absolutely nothing about dancing would be insulted. We want to see if our shoemakers can do solid, honest work-manship, not how good they are at self-promotion. An exhibition should be a festival of work, not of advertising. But hold on! There are three pairs of shoes that deserve the same fate, shoes that are made like ordinary outdoor shoes but with green velvet soles: one pair is even decorated with gold print in the manner of old book bindings.

We can rest assured. We Austrians will be stepping out into the next century in good footwear. And we will need it, because in the next century we all will be racing about on foot.

The American Walt Whitman, the greatest Germanic poet since Goethe, had prophetic vision of the coming century:

Have the elder races halted?
Do they droop and end their lesson,
Wearied over there beyond the seas?
We take up the task eternal, and the
burden and the lesson,
Pioneers! O pioneers!
All the past we leave behind
We debouch upon a newer mightier world,
varied world,
Fresh and strong, the world we seize, world of
Labor and the march,
Pioneers! O pioneers!

No, we have not stood still my dear old (friend) Walt Whitman. The old Germanic Blood still flows in our veins, ever ready to march. We too will do our bit to turn the standing and sitting world into a world of labor and the march.

(1898)

Ladies Fashion

Ladies fashion! What a terrible chapter of our cultural history, laying bare mankind's secret cravings. Reading its pages sends quivers of pain to one's very soul at the horrible perversions and unbelievable vices; one can hear the whimpering of abused children, the cries of mistreated women, the ear-splitting screams of tortured people, the wailing of victims, burning at a stake. Whips crack, and the air is filled with the smell of burning human flesh. Le béte humaine...

No, that is going to far. Human beings are not beasts. Love in a beast is as plain and simple as nature intended. But we humans abuse our nature, and nature abuses the Eros within us. We are beasts locked in a stall; beasts denied their natural nourishment, beasts that have to love on command. We are domesticated animals.

If we had remained beasts, then love would enter our hearts but once a year. However, our hardly repressible sensuality allows us to be capable of love at any time. We have been cheated out or our springtime and our sensuality is not simple, but complicated, not natural but unnatural. This unnatural sensuality erupts in a different manner in every century, and yes, even in every decade. Soon it is in the air and is contagious. It can spread through the country like a plague, which cannot be contained; sometimes it is like a mysterious virus, which the infected people know how to conceal from each other. Soon the world is full of feverish flagellants. The burning stakes take on the air of a perverted carnival, or this virus retreats to the most secret recesses of the soul. Be that as it may, the Marquis de Sade, the culmination of sensuality during his time, who thought up the most grandiose tortures conceivable, and the sweet, delicate girl who can breathe more freely once she has squashed the flea that bit her, are of the same stock.

The noble side of womankind has but one desire, to take her rightful place at the side of a great, strong man. Currently this longing can only be fulfilled if she wins a man's love. Love makes her subservient to the man. But this love is not a natural one. Would this be the case, she would confront him naked. But a naked woman has no allure for a man. Unclothed, she certainly can arouse a man's passion, but not maintain his love.

You will have heard the story that it was modesty that made woman adopt the fig leaf. How wrong that is! Modesty, a laborious emotion cleverly manufactured by cultural structures, was alien to the primitive human race. Woman clothed herself, and thereby made herself a mystery to man in order to fill his heart with a longing to solve the mystery.

The ability to inspire love is the only weapon a woman at the moment possesses in the battle of the sexes. Love, however, is a daughter of lust. A woman must hope to arouse a man's lust, his desire. A man can dominate a woman through the position he has achieved in society . He desires to be accepted among the elite, a longing expressed though his attire. Every barber wants to look like a count, while a count would never strive to look like a barber. Through marriage the man defines a woman's social status. No matter whether she previously was a high-class prostitute or a duchess, her own position is completely lost.

Therefore a woman is forced to use her clothing to appeal to the man's sensuality, unconsciously compelled to appeal to that pathological sensuality of his, for which only the social environment of the times can be held responsible.

It is apparent that changes in men's attire are brought about by the striving of the great majority to (at least) appear distinguished. Through this imitation they devalue the original distinguished styles and force the true arbiters of elegance – or those considered such by the people – to look for another style. The changes in women's clothing styles, however, are simply dictated by fluctuations in sensuality.

And our sensuality is constantly changing. Usually, certain aberrations accumulate during a particular period, to give way in due course to others. Convictions under paragraphs 125 through 133 of our criminal law[1] represent the most reliable of fashion journals. But, I do not want to delve too far into the past. At the end of the 1870s and the beginning of the 1880s the works of that particular literary school, which sought its effect in forthright realism, were full of descriptions of buxom beauties and flagellation scenes. I need only mention the names of Sacher-Masoch, Carulle Mendès, and Armand Sylvestre.[2] Soon after, clothes began to accentuate the voluptuous figure, the mature female form. A woman who did not have such curves had to fake them: *le cul de Paris* (Therefore the reemergence of the bustle). This led to a counter reaction. A cry for youth was heard. The child-woman came into fashion. The craving was for adolescents. The psyche of the young girl was picked apart and exploited in literature: Peter Altenberg for instance.[3] The Barrisons danced around on stage and into the hearts of men. And everything womanly had to disappear from women's clothing, in order to arm her for the battle against the child-

---

1 Austrian laws relating to sexual morality.
2 Leopold von Sacher-Masoch (1836–1895) and Austrian writer notorious for his novels and stories of perversion, the best known of which is *Venus in Furs*; Catulle Mendès (1841–1909), a French writer whose varied output included steamy" novels such as *La Première maitresse;* Armand Sylvestre (1837–1919).
3 A pseudonym for Richard Engländer (1859–1919), a Viennese writer, the archetypical bohemian. a minor French Parnassian poet, best known as the author of "Rabelaisian" tales.

woman. Hips were glossed over, and generous curves, once her pride and joy were an embarrassment. Hairstyles and wide sleeves gave them a childlike expression. These times too are now passed. But many will object and say that precisely at the present moment that trials for these crimes are increasing at a frightening rate. True. That is the best proof that they are disappearing from the upper classes, only to reappear at the lower levels of society. The great majority of men do not have the means to escape from this emotional hotbed atmosphere that those of higher standing have.

There has been one common thread running through this last century: the path to something had more appeal than the goal itself. The unripe fruit has exerted more appeal than the ripened fruit. Only during the last century did spring become the preferred season. The floral painters of previous centuries never painted buds. The professional beauties at the court of the French kings reached their prime at forty. But today, for those who consider themselves perfectly healthy – *consider* themselves, I said – that point is reached twenty years later. Therefore the woman will always choose the style that bears the hallmark of youth. Proof of this trend can be found in photographs over the course of the past twenty years by putting them next to each other. And what will she exclaim? "Didn't I look old twenty years ago"!? And, you will have to admit that she does look younger in the most recent picture.

As I have mentioned before, there are also parallel currents. The most important, the end of which is not yet in sight, and at the same time the strongest because it comes from England, is one that has its roots in the refined philosophy of ancient Greece – Platonic love. Women and men should be just good friends, companions. Fashion has accommodated this trend as well with the creation of the *tailor made costume*: the dress made by gentlemen tailors. In those circles, however, in which a woman's family background is important, in the aristocracy, where the rank of a chamberlain means that a woman's origin counts over generations, an emancipation from current ladies' fashion can be observed; the women are joining the men in the trend toward restrained good taste. People cannot get over their surprise at the simplicity currently en vogue among the aristocracy.

From what has been said, it is quite evident that the fashion trendsetters in men's clothing are those who hold the highest social position, while the leaders in ladies' fashion will be those women who have to show the greatest sensitivity in arousing men's sensuality, namely the cocottes.

Externally, women's clothing differs from that of men through the emphasis on decorative and colorful effects, and through the long skirt completely concealing women's legs. These two aspects demonstrate how much women have lagged behind the advances made in recent centuries. In no cultural epoch has there been such a great difference in clothing between free men and free women as in ours. In earlier times men, too wore colorful, richly decorated garments, the hem of which reached to the ground. Fortunately, the grandiose cultural development in this century has overcome the constraints of ornamentation. At this point I must repeat myself. The lower the cultural level, the greater the degree of ornamentation. Ornament is something that must be overcome. The Papuans and the criminals decorate their skin. The American Indian decorates his oar and his entire canoe. But the bicycle and the steam engine are free of ornamentation. As advances are made, culture frees one object after another from ornamentation.

Even today, men who want to emphasize their connection with preceding ages still wear velvet, silk and gold: the great aristocrats and the clergy. Men who are denied the modern right to self-determination are also dressed in velvet, silk and gold: lackeys and ministers of the crown. On special occasions, the monarch, as first servant of the state, cloaks himself in ermine and purple, whether they suit his taste or not. Not to forget soldiers in uniform, resplendent

ADOLF LOOS

in gold and bright colors, which help to underscore their sense of dependency.

The long garment, reaching to the ankles, is the shared symbol of those who do no physical labor. When physical labor and gainful employment were incompatible with the status of the free noble, the lord wore the long garment and the laborer the trousers. In China there still is the same distinction between mandarin and coolie (day laborer) today. Here in Austria the clergy underline, through the wearing of a cassock, that theirs is not a gainful occupation. Today the men of the upper classes have won the right to free employment, but on ceremonial occasions they still wear a garment that reaches to their knees, the frock coat.[4]

Society has not yet granted women from these classes the right to pursue gainful employment. In those classes where she has that right, she also wears trousers. One need only think of the women coal miners in Belgium, the dairymaids in the alpine pastures and the female prawn fishers of the North Sea.

Men, too, had to fight for the right to wear trousers. Riding, an activity employed for physical exercise but not material gain, was the first step. It is the knights who flourished in the thirteenth century and

---

4 In England, for audiences with the queen, the opening of parliament, weddings etc., the frock coat is worn, while in less advanced countries tails are worn on the occasions mentioned above, even today.

it is their love of horses that men have to thank for clothing that leaves their legs free. Even in the sixteenth century, when riding went out of fashion, could reverse that accomplishment. Only within the last fifty years have women won the right to physical exercise. There is a clear parallel between allowing the horse rider of the thirteenth century and the female cyclist of the twentieth the right to wear trousers that leave their legs free. That is a first step toward society sanctioning gainful employment for women.

The nobler side of a woman has but one desire, to take her rightful place alongside a great, strong man. Currently winning a man's love is the only way to fulfill this longing. But we are on the threshold of a newer, greater age. Women will no longer have to use their sensuality to achieve equal status with men, but will be able do so through their economic and intellectual independence, attained through work. A woman's value will not rise and fall with fluctuations in sensuality. Silks and satins, ribbons and bows, frills and furbelows will lose their appeal. They will disappear – and rightly so.

(1898/1902)

Short Hair (or not)

Let us turn this question around. Let us ask the ladies what they think of short hair on men. They probably will say that, this is solely the man's business. In Zurich, the director of a hospital fired a nursing attendant, because she had cut her hair short. Would it be possible for a female director of a hospital to fire a male nursing attendant for the same reason? Men wear their hair long for different reasons. The males of the Germanic tribes bound their hair in a ponytail, during the Middle Ages it was generally worn down to the shoulders, and only at the start of the Renaissance period, following an ancient Roman custom, was it cut short. During the time of Louis XIV it again was worn down to the shoulder and later braided into pigtails – yes, I am still referring to men's hair. During and after the French Revolution it was allowed to flow long and freely over the shoulders. The look even had a name: Schiller locks (in reference to Friedrich Schiller's curly look). Napoleon preferred the "Caesar" look. Today we would call it the "Eton Crop" or a bob. The women also cut their hair – why not? – and called it the "Tituskopf" (Titus look) after the curly, albeit shorthaired Roman Emperor. Why long hair is distinctly feminine and short hair distinctly male is something the "old women" among men should rack their empty brains about. To dictate that women should wear their hair long, that long hair creates feelings of carnal lust, and women are on this earth solely to provide this erotic tension is pure insolence! No woman would have the impertinence to reveal her personal erotic secrets due to a sense of moral responsibility. Women wear pants, the men wear frocks – in China. In the Occident it is the contrary. But it appears absurd to view these banalities as a divine order, or dictated by nature and morality. Workingwomen wear pants or short skirts: be they farmers or businesswomen. However, women who have little or nothing to do can easily let their clothes trail along behind them. But a man, who demands a woman follow his rules, only shows that he sees women as sexually dependent slaves. He would be better advised to concern himself with his attire. Women can deal with theirs quite well without male assistance.

(1928)

The English Uniform

Uniform in German means a "single form". The new government must not abolish this symbol of the old state – quite the contrary it must do its utmost to strengthen and deepen it's meaning. This corresponds to its social and nationalizing tendencies. The "one form", the uniform of the "Wehrmacht" (army) should not only be maintained, but even expanded.

The old government had attempted to force a particular military garment upon its citizens sworn to arms that was not in keeping with their sense of comfort or frame of mind. It also was not in keeping with their aesthetic needs and, therefore met with little success. To illustrate this I will quote a witty editorial salvo from "Die Muskete"[1]. "But gentlemen, please consider the fact we all are wearing the Emperor's jacket". (Standing around the major making this assessment were 10 to 20 officers, each wearing something quite different.)

The nervous system of the modern person revolts at the impertinence of being forced back twenty, fifty or even a hundred years. People who, since childhood, have marched in lace-up boots will hardly be able to march in jodhpurs (with elastic bands to boot)

---

1 Austrian satirical magazine published between 1905 and 1941.

– and that, despite the fact that the colonel has such a strong distaste for lace-up boots. (Here, it is important to point out that the notion of the regiment commander that this perspiration inducing footwear must be compulsory is completely unwarranted. These cultural aberrations were not even mentioned in any uniform code and therefore were hardly to be considered mandatory.) However, many obsolete, therefore culturally adverse, culturally inhibiting garments were the result of directives, thereby creating unnecessary obstacles on the path mankind is destined to take and robbed the inhabitants of the old monarchy of the liberty so freely accorded the newcomers. They wore "foot cloths" instead of stockings, waist belts instead of suspenders and so on.

One can only achieve uniformity when it corresponds to the identity of the person wearing it. It is imperative not to hinder the development of a person through his clothing. However, due to dictums of the old monarchy many old-fashioned people are still among our inhabitants, we must add: it is imperative for the spirit of the modern individual.

Let us take a look at uniform jacket. The English – a country where the highest percentage of modern, fashionable people live – elegantly solved this issue and all entente and neutral states have adopted this garment. However, there is a difference between the jacket of the officer and that of the common soldier.

This discrepancy too will disappear; it is only a matter of time. The officers' jacket will be the first choice because of its more modern appearance.

The jacket has a cut that ideally fulfills the two functions required of a uniform jacket: it is practical (therefore corresponds to the aesthetic requirements) and, thanks to this design requirement can only be made in this style. Stubborn unilateralism, dandyism, or other forms, due to size, too large, too small and so on are therefore rendered impossible.

The jacket is made like virtually any civilian jacket with an apportioned lapel. The hipbone provides the placement for the leather strap (overlap), which is defined by two buttons – one below and one above the overlap. Between the upper button and the top button of the jacket another button is sewn. It is the task of the tailor to insure a perfect symmetry between the two lower buttons, with the entire cut as well harmonizing with the distance between these other buttons. To serve as an underlay for the overlap, a cloth piece the same width as the leather strap is sewn in as a belt.

Four pockets adorn the outside. The upper two are for a small notebook and a handkerchief, the bottom two for larger items. Large breast pockets on men are unaesthetic and look absurd. Therefore the side pockets are that much larger – as large as possible. They start at the belt and go as far down as the cut of the jacket allows attached pockets to be. The breast pockets stretch from the upper breast button down to a few centimeters above the belt.

The design of the breast and side pockets is different. Both, as mentioned previously, are attached pockets. While the breast pockets only have a single middle box pleat (like the Norfolk Jacket) the side pockets are sewn on, much like "harmonica sleeves". Larger items can be easily carried within. On the backside, stitches can be seen. From the belt downwards it is slit – ideal for horseback riding.

Shirt and tie (with a knot) are visible. A suggestion: The old regiment colors could surface as neckties again. The collar is sewn on, just like those worn by our farmers – who thereby show more style then most city dwellers. Consequently, the neatness of the underclothes is insured without the need of an official order.

(1909?)

Answers from Adolf Loos

June 21, 1919

Question: Why are the sports trousers called knick-erbockers?

Answer: What Ms Vindopona[1] is for our writers and artists; the Knickerbockers are for their colleagues in New York. Father Knickerbocker is the personi-fication of New York. He is an elderly man with a three-corned hat (cocked hat), and full-bottom wig, buckled shoes and wide trousers ending at the knee (knickerbockers). He's that nice, fat tulip bulb grow-ing Dutch horticulturist of days gone by when New York was still called New Amsterdam. In Washington Irving's humoristic novel "A History of New York" its hero was a man named Diedrich Knickbocker. These wide Dutch trousers – still today the Dutch wear the widest trousers – were from then on called Knickerbockers, pronounced Nickerbockers or sim-ply termed knickers. The ancestors of the early Dutch settlers are still called Knickerbockers as well. The Knickerbockers Club can be compared to our Jockey Club, only it is much more exclusive. Roosevelt was not a Knickerbocker.

---

1 In reference to the early Roman military camp Vindobona, which was part of the Roman province Pannonia. Remains of which have been found in the center of Vienna. The local inhabitants were probably of Celtic and Illyrian origin.

August 9, 1919

Question: The crooked waist belt (Sam Browne) and star earrings.

Answer: I have received many letters complaining about my negative comments in my last answer column regarding these two bygone Austrian traditions. First I will deal with my aversion to star earrings. During the war when I saw our soldiers with their captured "Stella d'Italia" (Star of Italy), the five pointed star worn by Italian soldiers, and when I saw our street riff raff wearing these as well I could not suppress the queasy feeling that at the same time in Rome and Palermo the Austrian Officers Star was adorning the headgear of the same gutter snipes there. While one tends to endure the national disgrace at home, it is an immense embarrassment abroad and therefore unbearable for me. What must the Italians think of our officers! These stars, that not even a trapeze artist, in a better vaudeville show would wear, this earring spirit, which at the utmost should be worn by female circus riders, who in their carriages make village after village unsafe – children take the wash of the clothes lines, the comedians are coming – this is an ornament that a man, no, a soldier, anyone who has stood over a fellow combatant, one who calls himself an officer, who has this symbol sewn onto his uniform would dare wear! No! A person, who does not feel as I do about this, has no feeling for manliness, no feeling for human dignity. By God, our officers should be thankful for the people's guard patrols – even though they are illegal – that they do not go through life with an insignia that other nations would only accord to the *pauvre saltimbanque* (poor, street artist).

In regard to the Sam Browne one can already see by the position of the leather belt, there where the bayonet is carried, three cultural spheres: the German, the Austrian and the other nations. The other nations, including the Turks and the Bulgarians, wore their Sam Browne's horizontally, not askew. The military requires order, and an askew Sam Browne is sloppy. They were able to accomplish this by placing two hooks that were sewn into the side of the uniform jacket. The Germans, who also to a great extent value order, were able to attain this with two hooks as well, however, they did not look like hooks. They were intended to convey the appearance of buttons, sewn on in place of the two upper most buttons, which in total numbered six and adorned the tails of the uniform jacket. An imitation therefore, do you understand? By this I mean the difference between an honest hook and one that does not want to admit to being a hook, but something else. Why? Well, because it is pretty. Do you now understand the difference between a Turk, Bulgarian, etc. and a German?

The Austrian does not use a hook or attempt to feign order with a fake button. He is a straightforward fellow and wears the Sam Browne belt as it falls. Which means askew. And he is quite priggish about it – because it looks good.

August 19, 1919

Question: The end of the English moustache.

Answer: This headline that was seen in various papers these past days should naturally have been: The end of the moustache in England. Because in England no one actually knows what an English moustache is, or what an English moustache looks like. This is only known in Austria and Germany. The "English" moustache actually made its way into the world from Vienna and even came to England. Now it is true that it was the *common* man in England, the uneducated worker, and the day laborer who wore the neatly trimmed moustache. Never would a gentleman have had such a moustache. His was long and covered the lips, or as in the military, twisted into form with special grease. Unknown, however, was the *It is too much form*. It looked ridiculous, while the trimmed moustache looked common. The trimmed moustache made its way to Vienna with the appearance of the English stable boys. I, of course, am not referring to the jockeys whose social status is quite above such a common facial hairstyle. I am referring to the man who gave the horses water and groomed them.

Somehow it appears that for the Viennese an Englishman is a higher being, even if he only (is concerned with) shovels horse dung. One easily could be mistaken for one, if one were to trim one's moustache as short as he does. From the Vienna Freudenau[2] this facial fashion spread to the cavalry officers, above all in protest of the *It is too much form*, which was considered too vulgar even in our circles.

Even our aristocrats trimmed their moustaches and thereby made a terrible impression in England. However, soon there were a few courageous Englishmen who followed the example set by the Austrian aristocrats. But above all it was taken up in other countries. In England, because it was still seen as the typical *navie* moustache, it did not establish itself and, even today, is hardly worn. Therefore the newspaper article naturally meant that the moustache itself was disappearing and the cleanly shaven face was taking its place – as is the case in other countries as well. In a few years only the waiters and the valets will still be wearing a moustache. As a case in point, in France these have just acquired the right to wear a moustache.

---

2 The historical Viennese horse racing track.

August 23, 1919

Question: High Hat and Dignity.

Answer: The question is somewhat more extensive. It actually was: How do you explain the striving of all nations, during all times and cultural levels to raise the natural form of the head (for example in Egyptian mythology: Amun, Mut, Neith: the Aztecs, the helmets of the Greeks and others. Or, for instance, in the Middle Ages, the stacked hair of some African tribes, crowns and tiaras and, finally, the top hat) and to view this as noble and distinguished?

Actually, the question contains the answer in itself. For it is not a question, but rather a very perceptive observation, that has been obvious for quite some time. The question of headdress is pointless the instant it is not reserved for a special class. Anyone can wear a top hat today, however not a tiara. We must keep in mind that headdress, like the coat of arms, was reserved for the free man and that the slave had to do without it. However, since it was necessary for him to shield himself from sun and rain it was tolerated that he cover himself, but only under the condition that he remove it in reverence should he encounter a free man in the street. Even today this servile practice is still prevalent in our country. Only the English and the North Americans no longer employ this custom.

Perhaps one might raise the objection that in England and the United States upon a greeting, the head – however only in the case of offering a courtesy to a woman – is exposed as well. However, the significance of this greeting is completely different than in other countries of the Western World. It is common practice in these for the younger person or the one of the lower social standing, just as in the times of servitude, to greet first. In the aforementioned two countries it is the reverse. While a greeting here signifies I bow before you, over there it means: Hello, we know each other!

Therefore a completely contrary understanding of the greeting comes about: In our culture it is expected that the person of lower social standing greets first and the person of the higher standing appreciates the voluntary degradation of his counterpart, in the two *modern* countries the person of higher standing, which includes all women – children excepted – the right to choose their preference order for the greeting.

The higher hat, the raising of the status of an individual, has no purpose in countries that have had democratic governments for a longer period of time. If the headdress is still worn, such as the top hat, they are but relics of past centuries, like the button on a sleeve that allowed the rider while feeding or watering his horse, to easily roll up a sleeve. Today it no longer has this purpose, but the tailor still continues to sew it on. The different forms of greeting has possibly led to the greatest amount of misunderstanding, i.e. that the Englishman is arrogant and has bad manners. Should he sit at an already occupied table, he will not offer a greeting – for should he do so it would be an affront to his moral laws. It is difficult for us to understand this attitude. Perhaps it could be best explained by this example: the Englishman offers his hand first to younger man or one of lesser standing. Now this also occurs in our country, I have heard. Quite right, therefore a greeting in England is treated in the same way as a handshake.

September 20, 1919

Question: Whom would I wish to have in the audience for my lectures?

Answer: If I may, I would like to answer this question directly. Therefore, I would say all members of the government and those with such aspirations as well as social policy makers, educators and doctors.

October 4, 1919

Question: Does the latest men's fashion trend (the short English coat) have any relationship to the King of England?

Answer: Everything we wear has some relation to the King of England. Or, in other words, with the English people, because the English King is the visible symbol of English nature. He, therefore, cannot do anything that is contrary to this nature. However, what you mean by the short English coat, I simply do not know. Did you mean the *covert coat*? Or did you mean the average sports jacket. The first is worn, and has been since its first appearance more 150 years ago, two fingers longer than the jacket. And the jacket itself is currently worn longer as well and has a higher waist.

Question: My lectures.

Answer: Yes, they are the same lectures that I, to some extent, made under the titles, "About Standing, Walking, Sitting, Lying, Sleeping, Eating and Drinking" as well as "Learning How to Live at Home". I however, only recommend for those to attend who can do all of the aforementioned. Educators and physicians are welcome to attend. Wartime profiteers without any prior knowledge of the subject matter I strongly advise not to attend. You can, however, send your children, but that certainly would mean the end of your parental authority.

October 18, 1919

Question: Linen undergarments?

Answer: You criticize my lecture and come to the conclusion that these things are immaterial. "In linen underwear one also can be quite happy." That is quite correct, if you posses the nerves of an individual living anytime between 1780 and 1860. Should you however be so unlucky as to have the nerves of a contemporary person, modern nerves, then it is impossible. You probably will not understand this, as you have proven with your viewpoint that you are still wearing linen underwear – not knitted hosiery – and therefore have old nerves and not modern ones. But perhaps you will understand me better, if you imagine these lectures being given 120 years ago. The lecturer would have spoken about backward nations and condemned the fact that the Supreme Military Command would force their soldiers to uniformly powder their hair, braid it into a pigtail and to march about with gaiters buttoned over the knee. A like-minded person of the time would have addressed the same question to me and concluded that "even with a powdered pigtail one can be happy". It was possible – fifty years ago. But in 1800 it was not.

Dress Principals

For an artist all materials may have the same value, yet they do not have the same suitability for all his needs. Stability and the *producibility* require materials that are not in harmony with the actual purpose of the building. It is the task of the architect to create a comfortable and cozy room. Carpets are comfortable and cozy. He therefore decides to put one on the floor and to hang up a further four carpets to form the four walls. But one cannot build a house using only carpets. A floor carpet as well as a wall carpet needs a stable frame that keeps them in the proper position. The creation of this form is the architect's second task.

This is the proper, logical path that should be followed by the building industry, because this is how mankind learned to build. In the beginning there were clothes. People sought protection from the stress of weather, protection and warmth while sleeping. They sought to cover themselves. The blanket is the most ancient architectural detail. Originally it was made out of furs or handmade textiles. One can still recognize its importance in the Germanic languages (*DECKE, which in German also can mean ceiling*). This carpet must be placed so that it can provide enough protection for the entire family! The walls would soon be added in order to provide protection for the sides. And, in this order, the building concept was developed for mankind as well as the individual.

There are architects who do things quite differently. Their vision does not create rooms, but the wall frames. What space remains within these wall frames is then made into rooms. And, after this process these rooms are appropriately *dressed*. This is art on an empirical path.

The artist, the architect, first feels the effect that he intends on creating. He then sees the spaces that he wishes to produce with his mind's eye. The effects he wishes to produce for the viewer, be it fear or shock like in a prison; fear of God as in religion; anxious awe for the power of the state when seeing the presidential palace; reverence at a gravesite; a sense of home in front of an apartment building; conviviality as in a bar; these effects are created by the material and its form.

Every material has its particular form language and no material can make a claim on the form of another material. Because these forms have been created by the use and production of each material, these forms are unique. No material allows an encroachment into its form sphere. Should an attempt be made, the world brands it a fake. Art, however, has nothing to do with fakes, with lies. Its path is thorny, but it is pure.

The tower of St. Stephens Cathedral could certainly be cast in cement and erected anywhere, however, it no longer would be a work of art. And what holds for St. Stephens is valid for the Palazzo Pitti and what holds for Palazzo Pitti also pertains to Palazzo Farnese. And with the mention of these structures we find ourselves in the middle our "Ringstrasse"[1] architecture. A sad time for art, a sad time for the few artists among the architects of the time who were forced, by popular demand, to prostitute themselves. Only a few were lucky enough to find building owners with a greater vision; those who would let an artist follow his creative dream. The happiest must have been Schmidt, followed by Hansen, who in bad times sought salvation in terra cotta construction. Poor Ferstel must have suffered incredible anguish when he was forced, at the last minute, to cement cast whole sections of the façade on his university.[2] The other architects of this era, with few exceptions, hardly had such maudlin sentiments.

Have things changed? I would like to take on the responsibility of answering this question. Currently imitation and surrogate art still prevail in our architecture. Even worse, in the past years people have

---

1 A large boulevard encircling the center of Vienna along which many neo-classical historical buildings are located, including the Austrian Parliament and City Hall.
2 Well-known Viennese architects in the late 1800s and early 1900s.

come forth who actually defend this school of thought – one albeit anonymously, as this matter did not seem *clean* enough. Therefore our contemporary surrogate architect no longer has to stand shyly by the wayside. Now various constructions are nailed with aplomb to the façade and "side-stones" hung with artistic justification under the main cornice. Bring them on; the harbingers of imitation, the makers of adorned inlays, of spoil your home windows and the papier-mâché beakers! In Vienna a new spring is in bloom, the soil has been freshly fertilized.

Is housing space completely covered with carpets then not an imitation? The walls are not made of carpet! Certainly not. But these carpets only want to be carpets and not bricks and never want to be taken for anything else and do not show this in color or pattern, but show their importance by clearly dressing the wall space. They fulfill their purpose according to the principals of clothing.

As I mentioned at the beginning, clothing is older than construction. The reasons for clothing are multifold. Sometimes it serves as protection against the rigors of the weather, much like the oil paint coating on wood, iron or stone, sometimes for hygienic reasons, like the glazed stones covering the walls in the toilet. Sometimes as a means to achieve a certain effect, like the colorful painting of a statue, or the veneering of wood. The principal of clothing, which was first mentioned by Semper[3], also stretches into nature. A human being is covered by skin, a tree by bark.

However, based on this principal of clothing I would like to establish a specific law, which I would like to term the law of clothing. Please do not be frightened. It is often heard that laws signal the end of all progress. Then there are the old masters that did quite well without laws. Certainly, where larceny is unknown, it would be pointless to make laws prohibiting it. At a time when the materials used for clothing were not imitated there was no reason to fiddle about making laws. However, it seems to me that it is high time to do so.

The law is as follows: The possibility the *dressed* material can be mistaken for the clothing should in any case be ruled out. Applied in an individual case this sentence would be: Wood can be coated with every color, except for one – the color of wood. In a city where the Exhibition Commission decided that all the wood in the rotunda should be painted "like mahogany", in which this bastardization is the only paint décor for wood, this is a very bold sentence. It appears that there are people here that consider this refined. As the train and streetcar carriages as well

---

3 Gottfried Semper was a German architect, art critic, and professor of architecture. He designed and built the Semper Opera House in Dresden between 1838 and 1841.

as all other wagons come from England, these then are the only wooden objects that flaunt their autonomous colors. I dare to admit that I like a streetcar carriage – in particular those on the electric lines – in its autonomous color more than if it were to painted, according to the aesthetic principals of the Exhibition Commission, in mahogany.

In our nation, however, there too slumbers, albeit well hidden and buried, a true feeling of refinement. Otherwise the railroad administration would not be able to count on the factor that the brown, the original wood color painted third class, would awaken less refined feelings than the green second and first class.

I recently, in a rather drastic manner, provided proof of this subconscious feeling to a colleague. In a building there were two apartments on the first floor. The tenant in one of the apartments had the mullion and transom of his cross-window painted white instead of leaving it in the original brown spotted wood. We made a bet contingent on showing a certain amount of people the building and, without pointing out the difference in the cross windows colors, asked them on which side they thought Herr Pluntzengruber lived, and on which side Prince Liechtenstein, the current tenants of the two apartments. The result was concordant; the spotted wood side was deemed the one that Pluntzengruber lived in. Since this time my colleague only uses white paint.

The bastardization of wood naturally is an invention of our century. In the Middle Ages wood was painted a bright red, in the Renaissance blue, in the Baroque and Rococo periods interiors were white and exteriors green. Our peasants have managed to keep enough healthy common sense that they coat things in autonomous colors. How attractive the green gate and the green fence look, not to forget the agreeable green shutters matched with the freshly whitewashed walls. Sadly, however, some villages have apparently acquired the taste of our Exhibition Commission.

One will remember the moral outrage that occurred among the surrogate-applied arts camp when the first furniture from England coated in oil paint appeared in Vienna. The anger of these nice people was not directed at the coat of paint – for in Vienna too oil paint coating was employed the moment softwood came into use. But that the English furniture dared to present their oil coating so forthrightly and freely instead of attempting to imitate hardwood made the blood of these odd saints boil. They rolled their eyes and acted as if oil colors had never been used before. Presumably these gentlemen are also of the opinion that their bastardized furniture and constructions had only been identified as hardwood creations.

With such opinions pervading at the Exhibition of Painters I am sure that the cooperative of the same is thankful that I do not mention any names.

Applied to the Law of Clothing it would mean: the piece can have any ornament except for one – the bare brickwork.

One would believe that it would not be necessary to articulate something so self-evident, but only recently I was made aware of a building on which the plaster walls were in red and had white interstices. The popular kitchen decoration that imitates stone blocks is another case in point. And, therefore all materials used for decorating walls such as wallpaper, oil cloths, cloth fabrics and carpets, are used in such a way as not to allow bricks and stone blocks their rightful appearance. This also helps us understand why the stockings of our dancers appear so unaesthetic. Because knitted hosiery can be in any color, just not in skin color.

A material used for covering can keep its original color when the covered material also has the same color. Therefore I can paint the black iron with tar, I can cover one wood with another kind of wood veneering, etc., without having to coat the wood with a color; using fire or through galvanizing I can cover one metal with another. But the Law of Clothing forbids the use of a color that imitates the color of the material underneath it. Therefore iron can be tarred, painted with an oil color or galvanized, but never covered by a bronze color – a metal color.

I would like to mention the chamotte cement and cast stone blocks which on one hand imitate the terrazzo pavement (mosaic) and, on the other, Persian carpets. Certainly there are people who believe that the manufacturers must know their customers.

But no, all you imitators and surrogate architects, you are wrong. The human soul is something more refined and sublime as to let you fool it with your false ways and means. The prayer of the poor peasant girl in a church built with real material will rise more quickly to the heavens than if she would, with the same fervency, pray in a church surrounded by painted marble plaster walls. Our pitiful body, however, is in your power. Only five senses are at its disposal in order to differentiate between genuine and artificial. And there where the human beings can no longer reach, that is where your domain really begins, there is your realm. But once again you are wrong. Go ahead and paint on the wooden ceiling, very, very high, the best inlays – the poor eyes will accept it willingly and trustfully. But the divine psyche will not believe your deception. It can feel that even the best "laid" painted inlays are but oil paint.

The Woman and the Home

From north to south, from the orient to the occident the fame of the German housewife rings out. She knits her stockings herself, she is a regular subscriber to the "Gartenlaube"[1] and she dusts the furniture. And if lunch is to be eaten promptly at one o'clock, then the water is boiling in the kitchen at eight in the morning for cooking the beef. The eggs, for the "undressed apple strudel" are beaten into the flour even a bit earlier, because all these delicacies with which the German husband is fed take a great deal of time to prepare.

The German husbands, however, will be glad to hear that their French, English and American counterparts do not have it so good. Oh yes, particularly when I think about the American wives. One knows all about this clan. They loll about all day in their rocking chairs, smoking cigarettes. And what does the poor man there get to eat? Instead of the good, well-cooked (prepared over five hours!) beef these poor individuals have to eat steak everyday! Beefsteak, veal steak, muttonchops, pork chops and other pieces of meat just thrown onto the grill. Pieces of meat finished in five minutes!

---

1 German periodical popular in the late 1800s and considered the forerunner of modern magazines.

ADOLF LOOS

The American wives are even too lazy to knit stockings. They just go and buy them in a store. And they don't even bother with sewing clothes for the children, because should something have a hole in it instead of stitching it, they just go out and buy something new. They don't go to the market either. They have everything delivered to the house and pay the higher price for it. Oh, these spendthrifts! One can only admire our housewife. She is willing to travel for a day when necessary in order to buy a pound of flour two Kreutzer cheaper.

I had the opportunity to observe all this scandalous behavior first hand. Only the part regarding the rocking chair and the cigarette is not true. The Americans don't even have a rocking chair according to our definitions, and smoking cigarettes is not a vice known to women there. Even a man would not dare to smoke if he were in the company of a woman.

How did this part come into the story of the otherwise true depiction of the vices of the American wife? I thought about it for a long time. Finally I found the reason. What would the genuine German housewife, I mean the one that we are so proud of, not the degenerated sister who slowly has become Americanized do? I mean, what would this genuine housewife do if she no longer could travel for miles with the horse-drawn wagon to the cheapest source of purchase, would no longer knit stockings, not put on water in

the early morning hours and would not have her sub-
scription to the "Gartenlaube". She would be condemned to a life of lounging about and smoking cigarettes.

The American wife is far removed from doing
nothing. Apart from the aforementioned activities
she is capable of keeping herself occupied. She draws
and paints. She subscribes to *The Studio*[2]. She exer-
cises her eyes. The husband has no time for such
things. He is preoccupied with his job. Just like here.
However, since the wife here has no time for such
things, they are baffled by all questions regarding
art. There are enough questions regarding the household. Here a new oven must be installed, here the
room needs new wallpaper. There the furniture
needs new upholstery and, not to forget, a birthday
present must be bought for a favorite aunt. In this
case one can rely on the expertise of the salesman. It
is, however, terrible when one has to furnish a room,
an apartment. Terrible for the married couple that
feels compelled to furnish it on their own. Should
one buy this or that! Is it any wonder that they then,
disheartened, place a call to the decorator, the knight
in shining armor that deals with all these issues
according to his schemes and solves them with
aplomb to the satisfaction of all. Since they have

---

2 The Studio Magazine was an illustrated fine arts and decorative arts magazine,
founded in Great Britain in 1893. It had a major influence on the development of
the Art Nouveau and Arts and Crafts movements.

ADOLF LOOS

never learned to see with their own eyes, they are quite happy with the result. A blind person does not care if the room has green or red wallpaper.

The American wife is not blind. By knowing how to draw she understands form and through painting she has an understanding of color. If she has to buy something she does not have to rack her brains about it. She knows what she needs; she knows what the room requires. This self-assurance is evident in her home furnishings. No decorator crosses her threshold. And these rooms are filled with color! If one learns how to find the color tone prevalent in nature on the palette, when one is honest about one's intention and does not use the color tones of successful painters for one's own painting, then a new world of color and tone is discovered.

The worlds appears in a new luster, despite the jibes of those with stunted eyes, those who, instead of a lively eye, have a photographic device implanted in their mind and mock the blue trees and red skies of the seeing. A craving for color arises and one can, with certainty, still this hunger while the blind can easily get a stomach ulcer trying. Because without a confident feeling for color it is impossible to work with colors and, as a result, one runs the risk of showing bad taste.

There has been a great deal of mockery concerning the dilettantism of the fine arts. Some even feel that this has been harmful to art. What shortsightedness! Or, do you think playing the piano harmed Beethoven or Wagner? Their dear neighbors at the most. But this is certainly not the case when it comes to the fine arts.

Even without the nurturing of the fine arts the assistance of women in regard to house furnishing can only be welcome. A woman has more familiarity with colors than a man.

Color has not been banned from her clothing. Because of her preoccupation with colors in her attire she has managed to retain her color perception, something that is completely missing in a man's colorless attire. The decorator suffers the same fate as he does not really learn how to deal with colors, only with their transformation, which takes place over the years due to wear and dirt. Green turns into olive green and red turns into puce. And in this olive green and puce wallpaper sauce its inhabitants swim about for an entire century.

Résumé: the Austrian housewife tries to bind her husband to the family with good home cooking; the American and English housewives by creating a cozy home. This is also a result of the respective rivals lurking in these different cultures. In one it's the tavern around the corner, in the others it's the men's club.

Over the course of time, however, the German husband acquires a taste for English needs as well. He too, wishes to own a cozy home. And, therefore it would be wise for our housewives to Americanize themselves. A Viennese paper offers them assistance in this endeavor. I am referring to "Wiener Mode", the only periodical that gives the modern movement in the arts and crafts field its due – at least in regard to women's handicrafts. It's the only one of its kind in the German language. Hand in hand with the decorator's shop of Ludwig Novotny it has effected a revolution in needlework.

It has provided convincing evidence that needlework, which due to improper application was the poor stepchild of arts and crafts (one need only recall the parlor, which often conveyed the impression of crocheted museum), could also be used in great quantity in the living room. Novotny exhibited an entire room – I hardly dare say it, but very courageous indeed! – in the English style that consisted mainly of needlework decoration. Even though it was only an exhibition room it conveyed a warm and cozy atmosphere. Immediately one recognized that a woman rules here. And that is the correct impression. Family rooms should always have a feminine feel about them. That is a difficult task for the decorator. If he attempts to provide a feminine touch it turns into something slightly vulgar. Every woman has the ability to create a solid middle-class ambiance in her home on her own.

The knotted carpet is the latest addition to a woman's household interests. Over the course of the last years we have seen various very unsuccessful attempts at modernization. Even at the last Christmas exhibition a visitor was forced to traipse over a dragon battle motif created by a Viennese artist. Forty years ago it was battle of two lions. One can see that the form has changed, but the mindset has remained the same. Morris, the great arts and crafts reformer, tried his hand at carpets as well. No matter how hard he tried to create something new, it always gave the impression of an oriental carpet. The oriental carpet is the Acme of textile floor surface decoration. It has no figural decoration, is without obtrusive ornamentation even though it incorporates various colors and, by relinquishing the need for a long-distance and proximity effect, it represents the ultimate floor covering – *par excellence*. One was able to view various modern efforts by Orendi from the Maffersdorfer factory of Ginzkey. *Vivat sequens*!

The German home is still far removed from that wonderful English ideal. Our people sing marching, hiking and love songs. A song such as the English *Home, sweet home* they do not know. Words such as *homelike* cannot be properly translated into German. *Home feeling* is unknown. The children are very much attached to the family, but not to their own four walls. Moving does not give cause for melancholy in any family member – quite the contrary. One is excited about the new apartment and hopes to find more pleasant neighbors and a better custodian. That is the main concern. No one even considers the possibility that by having one's own home, one's own garden one could avoid all these unpleasant situations. Our time is crying for our own homesteads. Let this English illness also infect us as well, because currently the longing for one's own home is the primary driving force behind marriage. The bachelor of today can have virtually anything except for one thing: his own home.

(1904?)

About Thriftiness

A thing becomes outdated the moment our feelings revolt against it and we would appear absurd should we adamantly stick by this item of contention.

The top hat has various forms. Let's place 100 top hats next to each other. I wish to attend a funeral. I try on different hats, see that they mostly look impossible, even absurd and, finally, come to the conclusion that only one actually fits. The one, lets say, from 1924.

This top hat is ideal for me and my time, therefore the only acceptable choice.

People only find something modern when they think it is generally acceptable.

The top hat of 1924 is quite acceptable and if I could have worn it twenty years ago as well as I can wear it today, then everything would be quite fine. And because it is even possible for me to wear it, this top hat has fulfilled all its production, or in other words, its general economic justification.

But these are just fashion issues, which soon will pass.

But should it happen that a desk loses it aesthetic value for me, that I find it unbearable, then I have to get rid of it and buy a new one – however at a major financial loss.

ADOLF LOOS

I reject every kind of renewal obsession. Only the conservative person is frugal and every innovator is a squanderer.

However, a person who possesses a great deal of clothes takes great care to insure that these do not become unfashionable.

An individual who owns but one suit is not bound by any fashion concerns – quite the contrary. By constantly wearing the same suit he destroys it in a very short time and thereby forces his tailor to constantly come up with new forms.

The justification that these constant changes in fashion are a very useful thing, because it insures a great deal of work for the producer, is an incorrect point of view.

One needs many clothes so that they can be chosen according to the actual requirement. When it rains I take my rubber raincoat, in the spring I wear my overcoat, in winter a wool suit, and there is my entire wardrobe. Fashion is something that moves so quickly only because we just cannot make do with our things. The moment we have items that last longer and remain appealing, fashion immediately stops. We must measure beauty according to the principals of time. I cannot judge railroad tracks by how many trains can travel on them; I can only measure their durability. They will remain good as long as they continue to function well and reliably.

Material is alive. And material, fabric and a clothing product require a certain amount of molecular peace.

I therefore praise the large closets, which is the proper procedure, because, among other things, such a closet constantly reassures me that I am independent.

To change a form when it doesn't make any practical sense, or be improved on, is absolute nonsense.

I can discover something new, where there is a new challenge such as architecture: a building for turbines, or hangars for dirigibles – but a chair, a table, a closet? I will never admit that we should change centuries old, familiar forms, which are tried and proven because of the fancies of another.

The difference between the eighteenth century and the nineteenth century is nothing less than unfathomable. In the first, 95 percent of all people worked so that five percent could wear wigs and expensive clothes and act like squires. That was a great social injustice.

Today the worker and the English king basically, at least from the formal point of view, wear the same clothes. Our presidents and monarchs of the twentieth century do not have the least bit of interest in masquerades and traipsing about wearing crowns and ermine coats.

This has a deeper meaning than one would assume initially. The modern, intelligent individual must wear a disguise for others. This mask is the designated form of clothing for all people. Individual clothing is only for people with limited intellectual capacity. They have the need to scream out to the world what they are and who they ultimately are.

And so it is with furniture. A particular individual commissions arbitrary pieces to insure that others immediately know who the owner is, and that he as a person is completely different from all other people.

It is true that there are cheap and expensive clothes. This depends on the material used as well as the quality of the workmanship. However, this too has its limits. In sports we have champions who run the 100 yards in the absolute fastest time. There is one person that jumps higher than all others. Therefore there is one excellent tailor who uses the best material to technically make the best possible clothes. He could be in New York, in London, or in Paris – I don't know where he is.

Luxury is a very necessary thing. Someone must pay for quality labor. And the luxury industry, which serves only a few and basically represents the same concept as that mentioned earlier regarding the best sprinter and the best jumper means that a least a small group of manually skilled people must be able to produce this perfection in painstaking labor through talent and persistence. This must be the paradigm for the best human abilities. Otherwise everything in every field will spiral downwards. The tailor of the English king, through his inspirational example, through his consummate workmanship, influences the entire English clothing industry. Without this exemplary individual we would never rise above the average.

Every attempt to reduce the lifespan of an object is a mistake. On the contrary, we must raise the lifespan of the things that we produce. This is obviously the correct procedure.

Let's assume I have material of bad quality and commission a tailor to make me a suit with it, and the suit lasts a third of the time a good one would. A ratio of one to three! A good suit, this means thriftiness, a bad one means squandering money. This is a major and extraordinarily significant economic issue. When, however, items are produced using the best material and by the best-qualified craftsmen, objects considered to belong in the arts and crafts category that, because of their unconventional form, will in a few years appear dated are wasteful.

To spend months laboriously making lace, only to have the lace tear on the first night of use is a bad thing. Lace clothing can much more easily be made by machine and much cheaper.

Let us strive for refinement and be economical as well. I do not know who is thriftier: a person who drinks vintage wine or the person who drinks a vast quantity of bad wine.

But I wish to say something about the psychology of thrift. When I buy a cigarette case I do not want to be debased, do not want the enjoyment of the material and workmanship to be taken from me and replaced by the dubious pleasure of embellishment. I want the material to be appropriately used. A ring, this generally means a piece of high-quality gold in a circular form. A cigarette case should be two small, flat trays made of high-quality silver, completely smooth. The beautiful, pleasingly tactile, smooth silver surface is the best adornment.

But people do not like it. They want something complicated and protracted. Back to the Middle Ages!

This protraction, this complication! How can I enjoy a meal that has, with a great effort and extraordinary culinary ingenuity, taken eight days to prepare. This protraction, this complication and exaggerated attention turn this feast into something simply tasteless and absurd. The modern individual has a difficult time dealing with such an excessive waste of energy.

How can I enjoy an item that has taken five years to make? "This is male sadism". We are just too exalted to bother with such things today. We want the contrary: to save time, go easy on our fellow man and, above all, be thrifty with materials. I admit that

I am obsessed with frugality and wish to be a leader in thriftiness.

When I see a braced board, I feel sorry for this item because when I see the empty space I immediately imagine the missing piece. And I feel sorry for the missing piece.

In Prague I saw that precious material was ruthlessly cut and primed into complicated objects. This is a sin.

Every epoch is individually thrifty. In the eighteenth century there was plenty to eat, but hygiene was extremely neglected. It was a very fetid century. One can still even smell it today in the furniture.

The American soldiers even constructed bathrooms in their trenches. And what was the response? "These are supposed to be soldiers"? Why this reaction? Because, in Europe the idea of a good soldier is inseparably associated with a dirty soldier.

And once again it is evident that each individual is thrifty in different ways.

I am convinced that the proletarian is a much less thrifty person, that he spends money easily. The worker does not spend a great deal of time reflecting about drinking a glass of beer, while the civil servant spends a great deal of time contemplating this important decision. Yet, this same civil servant will, without hesitation, waste money on a silly decorative tie, a purchase the worker would spend at least half a day mulling over before making a decision. Before our love of embellishment we must have an understanding of the material. We have absolutely no knowledge of material. At one time gold ducats where thrown out of windows – a gentlemen's amusement – and pearls were dissolved in vinegar, which one then drank. Pearls were also cut. Today no one would consider doing something so sinful.

We even have less of a *feel* for material. The least appreciation for a substance can be found in a carpenter's shop. In architecture and carpentry the feel for material has been eliminated by the modern day architects.

A Chinaman was commissioned to do some work, he went into the forest to look for the right tree. He searched for a long time and, finally, he found it and said: "If I had not found this tree I would not have been able to do the work".

That is what I mean by a *feel* for material!

Material has to be revered again. Materials are truly mysterious substances. We must marvel and revere the fact that something like this has even been created.

Why then add an ornament to a beautiful, perfect substance? Using a violet wood stain to "improve" fine mahogany? These are criminal acts.

When someone tells me that it is a terrible punishment to be incarcerated in the average prison, which in itself appears quite pleasant due its simplicity with its white chalk walls and wooden pallets, I wonder how much more horrible it would be in a very contemporary penitentiary with an interior designed by a "modern architect" filled with his carpets, curtains, ashtrays, and clock hands – everything from the coal box to the penholder?

Give the designer ten years in this penitentiary!

Our architects, furniture designers and decorators, think superseding is their main task. Please, I repeat: supersede. The shoemaker who makes good shoes cannot supersede the good shoes he makes – never. And if I am fortunate enough to obtain a pair of his creations, I will take comfort in the fact that these will always be in fashion. Thank God that shoemakers do not supersede themselves. And may God keep architects from designing shoes. Because, should this happen then the shoemakers would, with tremendous zeal, supersede themselves every two years.

I have had shoes for twenty years and they still are not out of fashion.

I do not need to draw a sketch. A good architect knows how to write instructions for a structure. The Parthenon can be put into writing. I am against photographing interiors. Something completely different is depicted. There are architects who also design interiors not so that people can live comfortably in them, but rather that these look good on photographs. This is the so-called architecture draft that, through a mechanical combination of shadow and light lines, best correlates to a mechanical apparatus – in this case a darkroom. My house furnishings absolutely cannot be judged through photographs or reproductions. I am sure that, through the bane of photography, they would have no impact.

Photography actually dematerializes, but I specifically want people to feel the material in the room around them and have an effect on them. I want them to know everything about the room that surrounds them. I want them to become aware of each substance, the material, the wood, that they are able to embrace everything with their tactile senses, make it into a sensuous experience, that they can sit down comfortably and feel the chair over a vast expanse of their peripheral tactile senses and say: sitting here is the quintessential experience. How can I prove with a photograph, to the person seeing this photograph, regardless how well it is photographed, the feeling of how comfortable one sits in this chair?

So, therefore you see that a photograph alone expresses nothing. The photograph portrays appealing, or less appealing pictures. Through these pictures people are distracted from the essential thing. This is bad up-bringing. Photography is to blame that people want to furnish their homes not because they wish to live comfortably, but because they want them to look good. The photograph deceives. I have never wanted to deceive someone with my designs. I refuse to accept such methods. However, our architects have been trained only in these methods of deception and thereby become its protégés; they justify their reputation with appealing drawings and pretty photographs. They do this consciously, because they know that people are bewildered to such an extent that merely a photographic illusion is enough reason for them to want to live in, and even be proud of these surroundings. At the same time the customers are disingenuous to themselves and they certainly do not want to admit they are living in self-denial among all these drawings and photographs.

Folk art? What is it? Naked knees? Folk costumes? Folk dances? And those of us in the city, what should we do? Go to the theater, sit on benches and watch them perform? Isn't this completely absurd? Isn't it as embarrassing for us as it is for the country folk? Is this at all necessary – for us city folk and rural people? The borders between country and city should in any case fall. This difference is something artificial as well as absurd. We look upon the country folk as primitive people. For those of us in the city they seem ridiculous. In the country we city people are seen as ridiculous. By not understanding the basic functions of life, the lack of understanding for their work, the greater mission that every working person has and whatever useful task he pursues, wherever he may live, be it Paris or an isolated village in Moravia, we create an artificial border for which we should feel ashamed. These two people can have individual important qualities, because the Moravian is not fundamentally less of person due to his upbringing and the Parisian in turn can be a complete idiot, or one is successful and the other is not. In no way should the fact that because a person lives in a particular area of the globe, works as this or that, his qualities as a person be judged. Only a stupid person from Prague or Vienna can believe that he is better than someone living and working in Jihlava or Lhota.

I am always very happy when I can spend a greater amount of time in the United States or England.

The English bride would like nothing more than to carry away all her parents' furniture. In our country the bride will hear nothing of it. She certainly does not want to take any furniture off their hands, and thereby ease their financial obligation. She wants something new, something "fashionable", "modern". She even wants an "artistic concept". And, in four years, she will want another "artistic concept", because she will find that her furniture is looking very dated and new artistic designs are now en vogue. This is terrible! What a waste of energy, work, and money. This creates enormous economic havoc.

After all, English furniture is the pinnacle of comfort and ours – "designs based on the artistic concepts of modern-day architects" – a pyramid of utter nonsense and sins against material, purpose and workmanship.

An English wingback chair is absolutely perfect. Such quintessential models can be found in England and the United States in various other furniture genres as well. I believe that every year, around the world, only one good model is made that is capable of having an extensive (product) life. Everything else disappears in a few years and becomes as insufferable as a woman's old hat. The so-called arts & crafts industry really creates "back crippling" objects, and this so-called "artistic furniture" can only exist for a variety of wrong reasons: because it has been ordered and paid for beforehand, because it has been produced, because these items stand as a single set in a residence, therefore they patiently put up with them, regardless if they want to or not – even though they have been in a similar predicament before.

Therefore I do not like it when I am called Herr Architect. I prefer simply to be called by my name, Adolf Loos.

Thrift is something really terrible for the Viennese. It's truly an obsession when they have to redecorate, constantly buy something new, rearrange and run from one architect (interior designer) to another. This is a sign of our times – this chaos. Anyone that can make a personal contribution towards calming the current architectural trends will be doing a great service.

We currently do not have real architecture; we just have houses that are dressed up. This is like saying: It's not a saddle, but a dressed saddle – a saddle with an ornamental form, hardly adequate for its true purpose and virtually impossible to recognize under its artistic dress. It's comparable to a woman's body put into an applied artist's "designer" dress. We have to wear clothes, but why we have to *dress-up* architecture is something I just do not understand.

If the Ringstrasse had not been built in the 1870s and would be constructed today it would amount to an architectural catastrophe. I expect only one thing from an architect; that he demonstrate integrity in his building constructions.

I often visited Brno and compared the German house with the Czech "Beseda", the character of the two buildings immediately revealed what the future of Brno would be. It was quite evident! I would, in someway, like to reproduce pictures of these two structures next two each other. But, after what I saw in Prague recently I believe that Czech architects are being converted to the forms of the Brno German house. This is a bad sign.

A millimeter more or less in contour – this pains me. The contemporary architect, through his predisposition and his upbringing, is not a frugal person. And from those concerned with theater décor absolutely nothing sensible can be expected. These are people whose ingrained predisposition to extravagance with materials has become a habit. They evolve into specialists for cardboard rocks, dabbling in all kinds of illusions and sophistry, thereby completely losing their sense of dimension, because in theater nothing else is possible: everything is done randomly, only for the eyes. Theater directors have asked me to design stages. It is averse to my entire nature. I think theater architects are simply unbearable. This absolutely is not architecture.

In order to determine if something is modern it's best measured by comparing its compatibility to older things. I can assure you that my furniture goes well with European furniture of all epochs and all countries as well as with Chinese, Japanese and Indian bits and pieces. I dare someone entrusted with creating our "arts and crafts" to attempt the same!

Generally the first object in a room is the chair. If I intend to furnish something I first must have a chair and from it I then attend to everything else.

I think it is a great mistake when people acquire furniture made out of precious woods and expensive materials. They must always be extremely careful not to damage anything. To live really comfortably we have materials that, after all, will last us a life-

ADOLF LOOS

time and be they be nothing else but pigskin, oak and wool.

A residence must never be finished. Is a person, in a physical and intellectual sense, ever completed, finished?

Does a person ever reach a dead end? And if an individual is in perpetual motion and constantly evolving, when old needs are satisfied and new ones arise, when nature in general is changing and everything around as well, should that what is closest to a person, his residence remain unchanged, dead and furnished the same for all eternity? No. It is ridiculous to dictate to people where something should be placed and furnish them with everything from the toilet to the ashtray. I, on the other hand, love it when people arrange their furnishings how they need it (not I!) and it is completely natural, and I totally accept it, when they add their own pictures – their mementos, things they like, be they tasteful or tasteless – to their surroundings. This is hardly important to me. For many people these things represent sentimental moments and familiarity. This means that I am an architect that creates a human environment and not a synthetic, inhumane one. I am always amazed that so many people allow themselves to be tyrannized by so-called interior design architects!

At our academies our architects are taught, "how beautiful things once were, but how today, these things are useless". I too was a victim of this school of thought. And it took years before I was able to rid myself of these outrageous teachings, re-educate myself and to understand that essentially the aristocrat, in one aspect, can serve as a model for us all. I mean to say that he always shown a good sense for material. And I am not referring just to horses, or even beautiful horses, but purebreds – even thought they can be less compliant animals. It cannot be just any suitcase, but one made out of the very best material – a very solid one, to last for centuries. This is how I came to the conclusion that the principal of the, even though in other areas somewhat narrowminded, member of the Jockey Club is the correct one. The aristocrat's primary attention is geared to the material and the consummate workmanship of the corresponding item. It was a long and drawn out process before I finally understood this. Why? Because it was considered an ignominy to say this was the right way to think. By the way, Ruskin[1] is the one to blame for this. I am his sworn enemy. At some point in 1895, when as I was in America, I finally understood that a Thonet chair is the most modern chair.

Any carpenter can make the objects that I use to furnish a residence. I do not wish to be a "patent

---

1 John Ruskin was an English art critic and social thinker. His essays on art and architecture were extremely influential in the Victorian and Edwardian eras.

architect". Any marble worker, every textile laborer or industrialist can make my things, and does not have to beg me for permission. The essential thing being, that he does his work with integrity. Throughout my life I have kept away from nothing more carefully than the production of new forms.

The purpose of architects is to grasp the deeper meaning of life, to reflect on needs down to the smallest detail, to help the socially deprived and to provide the greatest amount of households with perfectly viable objects. Never should the architect waste his abilities on creating new forms.

But these are all opinions, which in the Europe of today, the number of people able to comprehend them can be counted on the fingers of one hand.

(1924?)

(Thoughts) About Adding Salt

Years ago I wrote on article about the way Viennese eat in restaurants. No newspaper wanted to print it. The newspapers were of the opinion if they did print it, they would immediately lose all their subscribers. I did however receive a proof of the article. It contained the following passage: "One of the more annoying aspects of Viennese restaurant life is the fact that one cannot add salt to the meals. There are no salt spoons. And therefore the table salt in a tavern, bit-by-bit, takes on the taste of the entire menu". I gave this passage someone to read, only to realize after he had read it how much he needed to read the whole article, because his response was as follows: "That is disgusting. Everyone uses their knife, on which scraps of food are still attached, to extract salt from the salt bowel. I always lick the knife off first before I extract the salt and add it to my meal".

It is clear to see that opinions on this subject differ.

In praise of a saltshaker.

It is quite strange that one can find more pleasure in the mundane, monetarily worthless, things of daily life than from more valuable material items. But why is it then that the loss of a handy pocketknife, or a well functioning fountain pen that suits one's hand so well can be so irritating?

Now I have a little thing from which I derive the greatest of pleasure. It is a quite common wooden, albeit innovative saltshaker, with a white lacquer, that I would not wish to do without at any meal. Like a small mushroom it stands ready to use on then table. I secretly wish, in contrast to before my owner-ship of this piece, that a meal is lacking in salt so that I may enjoy the privilege of using my little servant. It is not like the salt bowels of the past for which a knife was used to take out the salt, as no spoon was provided, and it is, thank God, not like the common saltshakers, were at first too little salt comes out and then too much. No, it is the perfect saltshaker. As I mentioned it is made out of wood, which extracts the slight clinging moisture from the salt. With this salt-shaker there are no clumps or other sticky hindrances and there is no over salting, because the button one pushes as needed not only strews the right amount of salt, but pulverizes and grinds the dried dry salt clumps. And this practical, pleasurable device costs only 1 Schilling 60[1].

(1905?)

---

1 Equivalent to about 1 Euro today.

Loos and the dancer Bessie Bruce (1913).

Adolf Loos: always well-dressed (1903?).

Loos and his bride-to-be: Claire Beck (1928).

Two of his major works: the American Bar ...

... and the "Haus am Michaelerplatz" in Vienna.

Credits:
Wien Museum: p. 7
Metroverlag: p. 124–127

Translation by Michael Edward Troy
Editing by Annita Seckinger

© 2011 Metroverlag
www.metroverlag.at
Verlagsbüro W. GmbH
All rights reserved
Gesamtherstellung: Druckerei Theiss GmbH, St. Stefan i. Lavanttal
ISBN 978-3-99300-040-0